K.ey

MW00698612

SMUGGLERS' TIMES:
Smuggling In The Days Of Marijuana Prohibition.

1974 to 1992

"True stories in a work of fiction."

As told by Keys Don and friends
To M. Dennis Taylor

SMUGGLERS' TIMES:
Smuggling In The Days Of Marijuana Prohibition

SMUGGLERS' TIMES:
Smuggling In The Days Of Marijuana Prohibition.

Our lawyer said to post that this book is a work of fiction. Names, characters, places, and incidents are used fictitiously. Any resemblance to actual persons, living or dead, events, or locales is entirely coincidental and the result of our imagination not changing them around enough. So, Feds, put down your highlighters.

Thank you to those who had confidence.

Foreword to The Book:

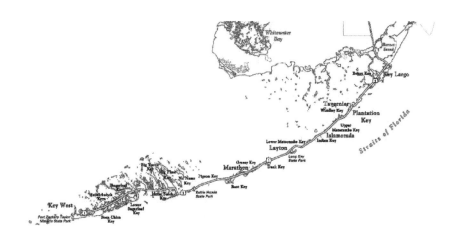

South Florida Has A History of Smuggling.

The archipelago of the Florida Keys begins just offshore of Miami and runs from the mainland out into the Gulf of Mexico, leeward of the Barrier Reef. Like a 150-mile long bracelet cast off a mermaid's delicate wrist, the Keys cascade south and west to Fort Jefferson, a Civil War-era fortress on Garden Key, once called the Gibraltar of the Gulf. To drive along this chain, one leaves Miami and heads 25 miles south to Homestead and Florida City, then off the mainland through estuaries and swamp to Key Largo and down US 1, the Overseas Highway, to begin island jumping over 42 bridges.

Originally built all the way to Key West for Henry Flagler's railroad to sea, one bridge was seven miles long, for much of the twentieth century it was the longest bridge in the

world. Mileposts count down from 108 at Jewfish Creek, in Key Largo to the much-stolen, mile-marker zero at the end of the road, in Key West.

South of Key Largo is Tavernier, so called because old charts of the area showed the channel of a natural, deeper-water creek connecting the Oceanside with the Gulf or Bayside of the island chain with the notation: "Tavern near creek."

Today's Village of Islamorada, or purple island, named in Spanish for the thorny bougainvillea flowers that grow there, includes Plantation Key, Windley Key and Upper and Lower Matecumbe.

Plantation Key, near mile-marker 88, is the location of the famous gourmet restaurant named for its address and is the island right in the middle of the stomping grounds of the characters that inhabit these stories.

Closer to Havana than it is to Miami, the famous tourist island-town of Key West is just ninety miles across the Gulfstream from the Cuban capital. An equal distance up the Keys is Islamorada, In between are thousands of islands and coves and basins and inlets and channels and places to hide. That's why the area has been a haven for smugglers since the times of the Spanish Main up until sometime late last night and continuing for as long as some people outlaw items others choose to make a profit from supplying.

The waters have been sailed by the famous and infamous, notably Blackbeard, Bogie, Hemmingway and Zane Grey. From pirates and privateers during the founding of the original colonies in the seventeenth century, to blockade runners in the Revolutionary and Civil Wars, rumrunners

during alcohol prohibition, migrant and refugee traffickers, marijuana purveyors, cocaine cowboys, and other contraband smugglers of today, the area is rich in the history of people bringing in stuff the government has said they were not allowed to import.

In the late 1960s and the 70s, an unpopular war was staffed by conscripted youth just out of high school. Forced to go to a strange and alien country, they fought an enemy that was often indistinguishable from the villagers they were sent to advise militarily, they found drugs were plentiful, cheap and immensely liberating from the hell of the theatre of war into which they had been dropped. Upon returning home they brought with them a taste for the marijuana and other substances they had used to escape, and an attitude of acceptance of herb as harmless and recreational.

In what people remember as a permissive era, the government also cracked down on rebellious protestors, dissidents and malcontents, when the establishment fought back with the "war on drugs," specifically marijuana.

Miami and the Keys, with a year-round mild climate, had an equally warm climate for newcomers seeking to make their fortune. Cuban refugees after the overthrow of Batista and then the Cuban missile crisis meant that soon a large part of the population was bi-lingual, breaking down a barrier to commerce between the area and Latin America.

CIA operatives were stationed in safe houses throughout the southern tip of the state plotting the Bay of Pigs invasion and seeking to overthrow banana regimes. All these provided a workforce to the smuggling trade. It was a perfect spot and the perfect time -- a window of opportunity, before the Drug

Enforcement Administration had their footing -- for the marijuana invasion from the southern part of the continent to the United States and Colombian Gold was the brand name of choice for weed, the best pot that had ever been available up until that time.

This is a story of some of the opposition to the authority's crackdown efforts. It is just some tales of people willing to risk their lives and liberty to bring back the goodies; for adventure, the high life and easy money in Smugglers' Times.

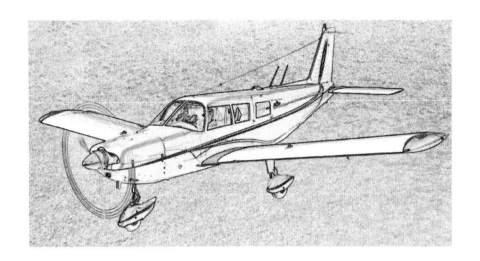

Prologue to Section 1:

For Adventure There Is Risk.

In 1958, at age seven, Don took his first pilot lessons – years before he was of legal age. In the cockpit of a single-engine plane, he sat boosted-up on telephone books. Before he had logged his first 45-minutes of airtime he was doing his favorite maneuvers, difficult hammerhead stalls. The local paper published an article on the fearless young ace who loved to spend time at a family friend's airport in Tennessee. By 19, Don had helped rebuild a light two-seater plane, called an Air Coupe and used it in South Florida and the Caribbean to log his hours for his commercial pilot's license. He was enrolled at Baker Aviation School in Miami, earning his airframe and power plant certificate before moving on to

oversee the maintenance and retrofit of a C130 that was the hurricane-hunter plane. It was about then that Don became aware of an even better way to earn a good living and retire young, by smuggling marijuana, flying a single engine plane on round-trips to Colombia to buy the pot, wholesale, making the equivalent of up to $220,000 in today's money for his share of a night's work...a long night's work that inaugurated a thirty-plus year smuggling career.

Introduction:

A Partnership Is Formed.

ISLAMORADA, Florida, with Don – "Marijuana is a people business," explained Don, a long-retired pioneer of the marijuana smuggling industry. Working under the name Gomer, he started out in the 1970s, flying single-engine planes back and forth from Miami, Florida to Ciénaga, Columbia near Cartagena becoming infamous in the business, carrying up to a million dollars-worth of pot per load, in today's money.

"I never got screwed by anyone in the marijuana business, like I did by partners in legitimate enterprises," Don finished with a sip of his signature vodka and cranberry juice with a wedge of Key Lime, then he added, "And I never brought in cocaine." He stated it flatly and with a sense of pride. "That's because I thought it was a nasty drug that did damage to society and people's lives."

"I bought it here, for my own use and my girlfriends' use, but I just bought some like anybody else would," Don went on, "I never *brought* it in…marijuana, you could get probation back then, a kilo of coke and they would put you away for years…and coke dealers would as soon shoot you, as sell to you."

Don is of average height and weight, always dressed in a typical fashion and has years of studied practice of not standing out. Being low-key and blending in was a great benefit in his chosen career, which began in the mid-1970s

and it fit with his stated motto: "I don't want to be famous, I only want to be rich."

In 1974, he was partners with Peggy, "she was not a girlfriend then (I'll tell you more about that situation later)," Don remarked. "She was married to Bob Z who is only important to the story for the problems he caused," that wound up moving Don's career along. Don said that "Peggy sold pot by the ounce and when you bought more of it, you could make more off each ounce. We sold it to friends, mostly. I'd buy her five pounds and she would sell it all and I'd get some more."

"Then Bob Z got into it and said he could get 100 pounds from Bear, 'on the arm' which meant you didn't have to pay up front…you could sell it and *then* pay for it." Don said that Bob Z had a purchaser in Columbus, Ohio and wanted to do the deal. "I said 'no' and went off to Sebring to the races," related Don.

Bob Z went ahead with the deal anyway and got busted. "Well, Bear wanted his money *any way*." His threats and the need to hire an attorney put Don and Peggy in a financial bind. A car accident a few days later left Don unable to work his day job, yet with some cash to pay Bear and the attorney; "but the partnership was ended, and I was about broke," said Don.

While still hobbling around on a broken knee from the accident, Don was at a local store where he happened to run into Chili, a friend he had known from high school. "Chili was a big guy, he was working unloading for a smuggler, named Jon B. -- an American -- who brought in Colombian pot… 'Colombian Gold' they called it back then," said Don.

"So, I started buying marijuana from Chili and we became good friends."

Networking was a key aspect of the smuggling industry. "The people in the marijuana business sometimes worked together many times and grew connections," Don related, "and Chili knew Roger, 'who handled sales.' Well Roger knew Bull, who spoke Spanish and had lived in Colombia for a time and was supposed to know his way around the area. Bull had a connection in Colombia to buy Colombian marijuana, is what I'm trying to tell you," related Don, summing it up. "We decided we were going to go get it -- in a little plane -- and fly it back to Miami," Thus a partnership was born and "our little scam was begun," Don said with a laugh.

"First, I'll tell you about the life of a smuggler, if we get enough good stories maybe we can make a book about them, maybe sell it for a mini-series or a movie. See, when marijuana is legal in a couple of years we will be like the rumrunners during prohibition and people might be interested in how it was in the old days. Then I'll talk about the *good times* I had along the way, because if you take a fall, the Feds are really good at taking away everything you have, but they can't take away all the good times you had spending the money that you don't have any more, but I don't want to get ahead of myself; and, remember, the whole story is *fiction*," he said with a pronounced wink.

Section 1

He Got Marijuana And Flew It Back To Miami.

Chapter 1

Preparations.
In 1975, Don Gets Ready for The Flights.

ISLAMORADA, Florida, with Don -- "I was living with a wild woman named Linda -- she's the one I bought the Corvette for, and she got wasted while having sex with this guy named Gary's wife and wrecked the 'vette on the way home -- well, as preparations for the flight, she and I went on a little vacation as tourists to Cartagena," Don laughed. "We rented a car and drove to Santa Marta, so I could scout the area and we only got lost four or five times."

Patriot Simon Bolivar, for whom the international airport is named, died in this sleepy village by the sea. In the 70s, it was a quiet hamlet between the mountains and the Bay of Santa Marta and was filled with quaint hotels and beach bars. Situated on the tip of the peninsula, near Cartagena, it was a favorite tourist locale and the picturesque colonial beach town became perhaps the hottest spot to pick up pot to bring back to the states.

"Back then nobody figured a single-engine plane would or could fly into Colombia to pick up marijuana and bring it back," explained Don, "because it was crazy! It was a stupid,

dangerous thing to do! But I had been more-or-less preparing for it my whole life." Don had years of experience flying the Air Coupe and landing on just about any semi-flat surface that looked interesting and he had virtually been raised in a plane, flying outside the boundaries of the law at a very young age.

Don rented a single-engine, fixed landing gear, Piper Cherokee Six, for a week from North Perry Airport in South Florida. He flew it to Tamiami Airport and removed the seats. Next, he temporarily added fuel bladders to hold 80 gallons of fuel and extend the range, so the plane could make it to Colombia. The fuel hookup had to be removable, so they could take it out later without it showing that the temporary fuel supply had been added. "The bladders turned out not to work too well and were dangerous," said Don.

"Bull went with me and he didn't work out too well either...I guess he helped me find the airstrip, which he was supposed to recognize because he had lived near there, but he couldn't find it when we first started looking," Don explained.

"We worried about safety, so we had maps and charts and compass settings, and a cheap raft and Vienna sausages in case we went down," explained Don. "Like anyone would have ever found us," he said. "In all the flights I never saw a boat or a plane, except once, it was just black." Even when Don was flying in daylight hours, it was decidedly vacant throughout the flight.

The duo left from Tamiami Airport at 10:00 pm. "It was supposed to be nine hours down, turnaround in about an hour, and nine hours back, so you arrived before sunset." Don said

that weather reports were not as good as today and there were none available between Haiti and Colombia anyway, plus there was no GPS back then that regular people could use.

The flights were to be low along the coastline, closer to the ocean surface than the roof of a five-story building. "Legally you can fly as low as you want, as long as you are 1000 feet from buildings or boats," said Don.

The flights were also slow, to economize on fuel consumption. Out over the Caribbean Sea, Don could fly higher, to avoid any inclement weather conditions.

"You would pass Haiti, turn right, follow a compass heading, and find Santa Marta, Colombia by dead reckoning." he said with a smile.

Chapter 2

The Maiden Flight.
The Best Made Plans Still Have Some
Wrinkles in Them.

The airstrip was on a banana plantation near a town they called Ciénaga, between Santa Marta and Cartagena. When Don and Bull arrived in the morning, they couldn't find the airstrip, despite Bull having lived in Colombia and being brought along for the specific reason of showing Don the spot to land. Eventually, people on the ground moved fence posts, chased away cows and Don could land. A truckload of heavily armed men greeted them. "They had all kinds of guns," described Don, "I mean automatic AK-47 kind of guns!" Other men quickly covered the plane with banana

leaves and disappeared, "but the guys with guns were always around, every time I went down there," said Don.

The landing was tough, with the props slashing up plants, but the real problem: "When we got there, there was no marijuana.

They had us wait in a hammock for six hours, with nothing for me to do, but watch the flies land on my belly, and very little understanding of what the hell was happening" explained Don who didn't remember this part ever being in a Jimmy Buffett song. "Finally, after hours of waiting, a guy rode up on a horse, holding the tail and back of a pig's butt," said Don, "it looked like he had just cut it off, and he cooked it over a fire and cut it into strips for us to eat."

After the meal, they smuggled Don and Bull to the house of a man who turned out to be the former mayor of the town. They crossed through military check points with Don staying quiet in the group, trying to fit in, despite having the straightest sandy blond hair for hundreds of miles in any direction and obviously not looking like a local. Then finally, they were welcomed to the home of "the old man" and everyone was glad to see the guys who came in on the plane.

"It took three days to round up the pot, and we stayed in hiding at the house; we didn't want to instigate questions as to what we might be doing there," said Don, "We got 400 pounds and it turned out to be the worst pot we ever got, because we were there in the wrong time of the year, afterwards we came after the harvest time in the fall."

The product was loaded on the plane and Don flew back. He barely got off the landing strip, and it took about 100 miles to get up to altitude because the plane was so

overloaded. When he got to Bimini in the Bahamas, Don flew 50 feet off the water, west for 50 miles toward Florida.

The tiny fishing villages on North and South Bimini are the original "Islands in the Stream," made famous by Ernest Hemingway's novel of that name. The deep channel between the sparsely populated, seven-mile long Cays flows so rapidly, old-timers joke that in days past, kids would troll for sailfish standing on the dock at Brown's Marina.

When he reached Miami, Don flew along the coast, beneath the buildings, then up to 1000 feet at West Palm Beach and out toward Lake Okeechobee.

Near Lake "O," Don landed on a dirt road close to a major highway, meeting Chili who was in a van. They unloaded quickly, then Don took off in the same direction and Chili headed out for traffic, to blend in with the flow.

"That way worked, but it presents a danger," said Don, "because you can't control who is around on the dirt road." He added, "I decided I didn't need a co-pilot and especially not Bull and I always flew alone after that." The product was sold to them "on the arm." Don remembers earning $25,000 for his cut for about a week's work. That's over $110,000 in today's money. Hubert, Ignacio (Iggy) and Bob bought the entire load, making sales of the product easy. Future flights got even more lucrative.

Chapter 3

Temporary Tank Fuels Flight Problems.
The First Trip in 1975, In a Cessna 206.

The second trip, the team applied the new knowledge they had gained from the maiden flight. Don rented a Cessna 206 at North Perry Airport for a two-week period with the plan of making two flights during that time. With the added cargo capacity, Don's share for the two trips turned out to be $100,000 then, marking the first year his efforts put him in six figures. That equates to over $440,000 today!

Don treated himself to his favorite wine and bought a case of Chateau Lafitte Rothschild, 1970 vintage. It became a tradition, "every time I made $100,000 I bought another case," recounted Don.

The Cessna 206 is marketed as a station wagon type of aircraft. It is designed to carry heavy weight and have a short takeoff. Don flew it at about 150 mph.

Again, Don first headed to Tamiami Airport and followed the same procedure of removing the seats. Only this time he temporarily added an 80-gallon, aluminum fuel tank he had a vendor fabricate, telling him it was "for his boat," so the vendor wouldn't have any suspicions as to how the tank was really to be used. He placed the tank behind the pilot's seat, the only seat in the plane.

"We filled the plane so full of marijuana that I removed the wheel and poked a hole in the bundle in the co-pilot's area, so I had full travel of the controls," said Don. The pot wasn't bundled in burlap, you do that on boats, I didn't want

the weight of the burlap on my plane, we used plastic wrap because every ounce counted," he explained. "I did this little trick with the controls on both of those [rented Cessna 206] flights and carried about 900 pounds of pot," said Don. The product was piled up so that he could only see out part of the front window and to his side, but the trips helped fine-tune his skills of flying economically.

On the way back, he burned the fuel in the temporary tank first. This created a problem, "the plane became tail heavy," and it moved like a porpoise undulating up and down all the way back, explained Don. Chili met him when he landed on a dirt road in rural West Palm Beach, and the tail was almost dragging. "After we rushed around and unloaded the marijuana into Chili's van, when I took off, we had left the seatbelt hanging out the backdoor, so I had to crawl back while the plane was flying and open the door to pull the seatbelt in, so it wouldn't damage the plane. Then I had to get back up to my seat to level the plane. I always checked the seatbelt after that." More lessons learned.

"The marijuana was excellent quality Colombian Gold worth over $250 per pound which was up from the $200 per pound that the first load had yielded," said Don, speaking about 1975 dollars.

For the second of the two trips in quick succession, step one was to put the fuel tank further up, next to the pilot's seat. "And I burned that fuel closer to home," said Don, "so the plane flew fine."

Chapter 4

Two Jets Make A Surprise Appearance.
The Second Trip in a Week.

There are times when two things happen so closely together that you always remember them as a single action. That's what happened on this quiet, moonlit night with the lights of Cuba off in the distance. The radio was on the emergency channel, when the message broke through in English: "Aircraft in Cuban air space maintain 12 miles off Cuba," as a MIG flew directly in front and another over the top of Don's plane; "That got my attention!" he laughed, "I cut left and then farther left," apparently the lights of Cuba had not been distant enough."

"Flying along at night -- it was BLACK -- the planes had a wing leveler, but not a good auto pilot," Don explained, "you had to keep track of the altitude… not believing the instruments is what still gets pilots killed."

When it was quiet, a pilot was alone with just their thoughts… and all the phantom noises they heard from the plane. Don said that "you could talk yourself into all kinds of engine problems that you thought you heard, especially in the area between Haiti and Colombia."

Except for the buzz by the MIGs, this flight was smooth and profitable. Yet, Don was totally burned-out and needed a break. He told his partners that, "We needed to buy our own plane."

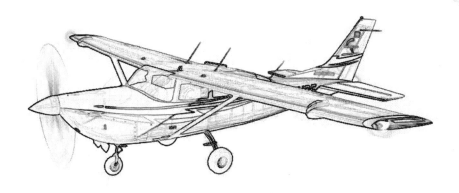

Chapter 5

The Partners Buy Their Own Plane.
The First Flight of 1976.

Don bought a Cessna 206 and took about seven months off to have it modified with wing tanks and a 60-gallon, aluminum auxiliary fuel tank specifically outfitted for his needs. This plane could carry 1000 pounds of marijuana. He also bought "the ranch," 40 fenced-in acres, west of Stuart, Florida out by Lake Okeechobee, four miles down a dirt road, but near a major thoroughfare with plenty of traffic for a van to get lost in. It had a small, but nice house and plenty of controllable privacy.

At the ranch he had to have the land smoothed out to fill in all the Armadillo holes. "I didn't even know there were Armadillos in Florida," laughed Don, "and now they were keeping me from landing a plane."

For the most part, Don flew to the home with friends to watch Dolphin football games that were blacked out in Miami

– except for two flights when he came in from Colombia and his cargo was a million-dollars-worth of marijuana.

On the first of these flights, on the way down to Colombia, Don was "south of Haiti, under a full moon when it got very black, with hail beating down on the plane like it was going to break the wings off. Suddenly the plane lost 2000 feet of altitude, then gained 2000 feet; the gas tank crashing up and then down…that also got my attention," related Don.

"In the morning when I landed on the airstrip in Colombia, there was a DC-3 broken down at the end of the airstrip, so I parked next to its wing," said Don. The twin-engine, 21-seat, DC-3s were first built in the mid-30s as commercial, freighter and military aircraft and thousands were built under license, around the world for decades. This freighter was a considerably larger aircraft than the six-seater Cessna 206 that Don and others landed on the banana plantation. "Obviously they are no longer worried about hiding the airstrip," Don thought to himself.

They came out to load the pot and empty his gallon milk jug of pee, which he had accumulated during the trip. "I drank beer along the way to calm my nerves, and always had a full jug, the most pee they ever saw," laughed Don. "I brought back 1000 pounds of marijuana, [with the obstructed view out the windshield] you could only see directly out the front and to your side, so it made it tough to see where you were landing."

The trip went as planned, with no major problems and with a smooth "touch down" at the ranch that evening.

Chapter 6

The Final Trip by Air.
Trip Number 5, in 1977.

At the time Don didn't know that trip number five was *the* last trip, he just knew it was *his* last trip. He planned on hiring pilots to carry on in his place because he had so many other things to do in the expanding business.

In the morning when he sighted the airstrip, the same DC-3 was still there, still awaiting its needed part to make the repair. Thunderstorms and squalls were moving in when he left and on-the-way back he never got over 1000 feet, "so I couldn't get over the squalls, and had to fly around the rainstorms, it took 11 hours to get back," explained Don.

He was so burned-out that he wanted at least a year off and a twin-engine plane for the business. He began formulating how to adapt this plane and knew just which one to modify to make the smuggling craft. He wanted a twin-engine Navajo, modified to fly 1100 miles non-stop, and carry 1000 pounds with only one of its engines running.

The flights to the ranch to watch the Dolphin games were also an opportunity to find out if any authorities had the place under surveillance. One gameday, Don found out it was indeed being watched, when "the cops showed up to check out the plane." It was completely clean, but he never made another smuggling flight to the ranch. Technology was changing, and Don was ready to move on to a new way of getting bigger loads of marijuana into South Florida – using boats.

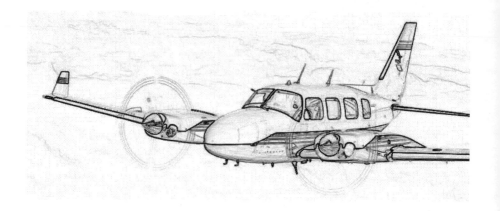

SIDEBAR 1

Don's Dream Plane.
The Cowboy's Piper Navajo Panther
is Still Smuggling Today.

In the hours of flying alone, with just WQAM on the Radio Directional Finder, Don would sometimes think about the kind of smuggling plane he really wanted. Based upon the challenges he had faced in his own personal experience, he had some very specific ideas.

Don had said, half teasing, that "if a twin-engine plane loses an engine, you're going down, it just may take a while," so he flew single engine planes because "there were only half as many engines to break." He knew he wanted a twin-engine plane that could carry a 1000-pound payload with only one of the engines running. Don wanted a Piper Navajo, in production since 1967, and he would modify it to fly 1100 miles non-stop and carry that 1000-pound load with only one of its turbocharged engines running. He wanted it to have

short propeller blades because he was landing on banana plantations and he needed it to take off quick for short runways, and he wanted it to be as quiet as possible – so as not to "disturb the neighbors."

Don knew just where to work out the logistics and flight experiments with these modifications. He had a lifelong family friend who owned an airport and Don sent him a deposit for a Navajo to work the transitional magic on.

Taking almost a year off to work on the plan, Don's plane became a legitimate conversion offered by Don's friend and over the years "it made him legitimately very rich," said Don. Dubbed a Navajo Panther in sales literature by the company, the 1978 plane took on a distinctive look with "a blunter nacelle, with deeper inlets" that could scoop in more air to cool the engines. Don said they had "a boat builder fabricate wing tips that turned up, extending almost two feet," effectively lengthening the wings and creating more lift and stability, and even reducing yawing in turbulent air. Shorter, four-blade props and wider spinners had blade tips where their last half-inch were bent back 90 degrees. "That was an old trick the friend had learned during the war," to quiet the noise of the engines," explained Don.

"The plane was perfect for smuggling and coke smugglers are still using it today," recounted Don, "Hell, Barry Seal's crew flew one in the movie American Made." Ironically, Don never used the plane to smuggle. He chose to switch to boats and stay with marijuana as his product. Don's vision of the Navajo Panther was purpose-built for 1000-pound loads and became the cocaine runners' favorite.

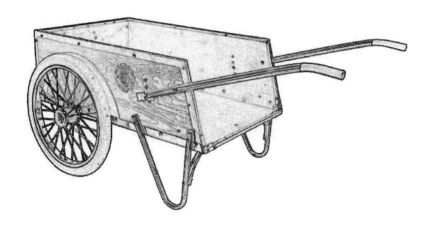

Prologue to Section 2:

The Difference Between A Pirate and A Merchant.
Who Is in Charge.

The pirate profession may not be as old as prostitution, but one can bet that shortly after discovering that loads are easier to carry when they are floated, someone found out that people had a desire for things that were hard to get, so the two concepts got together. The difference between merchant trade and contraband is who is in charge. Don decided to move from the air to boats because the wager was about the same compared, to the risk to life and liberty, but boats carried a whole lot more merchandise. He moved to power boats to off-load, then got an off-load house right on the water. With a seasoned crew the procedure was eventually set up like a machine.

Section 2

They Would Buy And Load The Marijuana,
Then Get It Into Florida.

Chapter 7

Sea Voyages on Ships Stacked with Weed.
The First Trip on the Sweetie Pie.

ISLAMORADA, Florida, with Don and Butch -- Don, Chili and Roger agreed with Jon B to make three smuggling trips using his 43-foot, motor-sailor, the Sweetie Pie. Chili knew Jon B from his own off-loading days, so the deal was simple enough. Don or Chili would load the boat using their same connections in Santa Marta and Jon B's captain would transport the marijuana to near Alligator Light, off Islamorada, where Neil, the Whalebone's off-loading crew would get it in, and up US 1 to stash houses Roger had organized in the Redlands, a rural area southwest of Miami. They would split the load fifty-fifty for the tasks of buying and loading the marijuana, and then getting it into Florida to the stash houses.

The Redlands are at the foot of the Florida mainland, just up a dark, curving 18-mile, two-lane stretch of US 1 known as "death alley." It was notorious for head-on collisions and cars winding up in the canals on either side of the narrow road that were dug to get fill for the roadbed. The load would

be brought up US 1, and then the driver would cut back onto Route 27 into the Redlands.

It was the perfect place to go for smugglers' stash houses. The agricultural area was filled with lush nurseries, homes on thickly landscaped five-acre parcels, remnants of citrus groves and fences: electric fences, wooden fences and gated properties. Everyone had privacy, and no one paid too much attention to other peoples' business. There was plenty of traffic: trucks and pick-ups and step vans. "The Redlands was set up perfect for smuggling," said Butch, "people try to bring in their loads at ritzy resorts like [nearby] Ocean Reef, that's problems, those people are nosey."

"It turns out we only made two of the trips, then I said there was no way in hell I'm going to work like that again," said Don. "I didn't like the way they did some things."

This is where Don first came into contact with Butch. The two merely knew *of* each other as all of the different tasks involved in smuggling were highly compartmentalized with guys trying *not to know* each other. Don was working as Gomer, a somewhat aloof partner and Butch, whose name wasn't Butch either, was becoming a resourceful and reliable off-loader. "Nobody used their real names," said Don, "but Gomer finally got to be too famous and I had to kill it off and stop using the name."

"In the seventies, everybody in the Keys had their own little scam going, or at least had been recruited," said Butch, who had a sail-loft with his partner, college-buddy and frat-brother, Otis, where the Worldwide Sportsman is now, in Islamorada.

Butch lived on his Chinese Junk, moored out back in Little Basin. He had retailed pot in college before moving to the Keys, looking to make some "wholesale weed connections."

"One day a mutual friend introduced me to Neil, the Whalebone, who asked me if I knew how to sail and if I'd like to make $10,000 that night."

"Fuck yeah, on both accounts," Butch said, "and I got into off-loading the Sweetie Pie."

The Sweetie Pie was a Sparkman and Stevens-designed, 43-foot, twin diesel engine, steel, single-mast, motor-sailor, which sailed, "but not well." It was a really tough boat that had been used, abused, ignored, worked-hard "and put away wet," said Butch.

When a scam was over, the Captain and crew scattered, and the boat was just left. "So, there were constantly maintenance issues from it just sitting with no attention," explained Don.

The first leg of the first trip of the Sweetie Pie left out of Miami and cut through Gunn Cay and Cat Cay, across the Great Bahama Bank, to Nassau, where the starter went out.

Don was the only one with a mechanical background and while not actually a diesel mechanic, he was the closest they had, so he flew over to fix the boat. The duty and shipping about doubled the price of the parts, "but I finally got it running," remarked Don. He again had to become the fly-in mechanic when the boat had generator problems and pulled into Aruba.

Chili, who could speak Spanish, went down to Colombia to load the boat. At the time, Santa Marta was the place to get

marijuana to bring into the states "and we already had great connections," explained Don.

Either Chili or Don or their surrogate was there to load every boat. It helped to make certain everything went smoothly and according to plan. Butch explained "crews want to be able to talk to a gringo they know."

Butch's gig for that first $10,000 night was to motor a 24-foot, shallow draft sailboat, called a Terrapin, out to pick-up a load. He was on one of three of the beat-up old sailboats that went to the Sweetie Pie. The fourth or backup boat was Don's 24-foot Lone Star, aluminum weekend cruiser.

The reason for the extra, backup boat was because they were never sure exactly how much pot the Columbians would send. They would load the boat until it was full or send as much as they had. Any that wouldn't fit onto the off-load boats had to be disposed of at sea. This was literally throwing away pure profit right into the ocean. So, an unused boat on hand was a smart way to maximize the value of the load.

Bales floating around also left a beacon, so to speak, "a calling card for the authorities that an off-load had taken place in the neighborhood," said Butch. There was no good reason to waste profit and bring heat down on the area when more work was to be done.

The boats were tied up alongside of the Sweetie Pie and loaded with two- to three-thousand pounds of marijuana, then sailed back to shore. Butch's boat went to a house on Lower Matecumbe Key that had a boat ramp. The property had been rented by Neil, the Whalebone, from a university president, so the house had a good pedigree and cool neighbors who had

their own stuff going on and were not overly curious about some noise here and there.

The route took Butch and Neil through a narrow, little mangrove wheel pitch, a natural channel that was a mile-or-more-long. It was only a few feet deep and not much wider in some points than the boat. At the bridge between Bud and Mary's Marina and Robbie's Marina, they lowered the mast, crossed under, then re-stepped the mast, and anchored behind Indian Key, waiting for a call on citizen's band or CB radio. "We talked like we were truckers or cars moving down the highway," said Butch. "We'd ask them to 'turn your porch light on, good buddy,' to get them to flash their bow lights." Each boat had a specific handle or codename. The monikers were the Whalebone, Jack knife, and Slingshot.

Butch was on the Whalebone as they waited behind Indian Key. When they were alerted, the 9.9 horsepower Evinrude outboard could get them out to Alligator Lighthouse at the reef in 45 minutes.

There was no one around and for the most part the seas were calm, and the trip out went "smoothly." "Except for the bit where it was tied up to the Sweetie Pie, which never anchored, and it got crushed under the port side of the boat, blowing out the windows and smashing in the hull," recounted Butch.

The Terrapins were loaded to the gunwales with about a ton and a half of pot for the trip back. We just used the jib or the engine, never the main," explained Butch. "We didn't even have a boom."

Built by legendary Keys boat designer Dave Westphal, Terrapins were shoal draft vessels crafted for local shallow

waters and had a large amount of space between the waterline and the top of the side of the boat. Butch explained that "this free-board looked normal when the boat was loaded." The Terrapins were inexpensive Keys cruisers.

Another trick the smuggler's used was to paint the bottom color up higher on the side of the hull, so a boat riding low with a load still looked like it had the right waterline.

The Terrapin was brought back to the university president's house and tied up until daybreak, when it was loaded back onto its trailer. The other two boats went to public ramps to be pulled out onto trailers.

Butch recounted that it took two pick-up trucks to pull the loaded boat and trailer out at the ramp. "The first time we pulled it out, a big branch that no one noticed caught the mast just below the spreaders and yanked the whole boat off the trailer. It bounced once on the ramp and then went back into the water. It did some more damage to the boat and bent the trailer."

"The crew all looked at each other for a moment, wondering just who was the one who was supposed to have been watching for tree branches?" remarked Butch.

"We were shocked, to say the least," explained Butch, "What should have been a pretty simple job had just gotten a lot more complicated, plus, all the commotion of two trucks chained together and trying to get the boat on a bent trailer was starting to create a scene."

"We had to hurry, and then clean the boat up and make some on-the-spot repairs to get it looking presentable enough to tow it to a mall in Homestead, where they dropped the rig off in the parking lot," said Butch.

SMUGGLERS' TIMES:
Smuggling In The Days Of Marijuana Prohibition.

30

It was then picked-up by the stash house crew, who never met the off-loaders. The stash house crew did their job and returned the empty boat and trailer to the parking lot at the mall to be picked back up.

"Nobody was supposed to know anybody they didn't have to know," explained Don, "so if they got caught, they didn't know anyone to tell on, and except for when they actually had the pot, they were not at risk for being arrested," explained Don.

"Which is stupid that you could even get in trouble for it," remarked Butch. "It is a victimless crime, you sell pot and both parties are happy, no one got hurt. I think it was because it was all tax free. That's what they hated! It's just crazy the way the laws were. But now that's changing."

In those days of smuggling, communications were always a problem. To talk to Colombia, it was not uncommon to go to a phone booth with $30 in change. "The connections were bad, and it took a long time to get through," said Don.

It took two to three weeks by boat to Colombia because they stopped along the way and then about a week to 10 days to get back travelling non-stop, and there was no satellite phone or any kind of communication with a boat while it was at sea. When they were within 20 miles of either end of the trip they could use VHF radios, but ten, nerve-racking days was a long time to be out of contact with the load.

That first trip the Sweetie Pie was five days late arriving at Alligator Light. It brought in 7000 pounds of pot that cost $50 to $75 per pound from the Colombians and sold for $200 to $250 per pound for a total of about $1.4 million before expenses. These included the fee for the off-loaders, which

was $10,000 per person for eight people; $35,000 to $50,000 to prepare the boat, and stock it with food and fuel; and even just the food was about $5000 and that increased with delays.

Everything could cause a delay: mechanical problems, connection communications, acquiring the marijuana, even the weather could cause a delay. "You don't want to load in the rain because you don't want wet weed," said Butch, "when it gets wet, it gets an ammonia smell to it and the value drops by about half."

"I got paid in pot, beautiful Colombian," remembered Butch, "then I transported it to Bloomington, Indiana... I could carry 350 pounds on a trip and I made $30,000 more for the extra risk and effort." These amounts can be multiplied by about four and a half to express the value in today's dollars. Don continued to treat himself every time he made over $100,000 by purchasing a case of Chateau Laffite Rothschild, 1970 vintage.

Chapter 8

Screw Ups on The Sweetie Pie's Second Trip.
The Final Straw.

Don said that it took about six months to sell the pot, collect all the money, rehab and refit the boat and organize the next trip. When it came time for its second trip it seems hard to explain just how nasty and worn out the Sweetie Pie had become in her final months. The captain and crew virtually abandoned her at the end of each caper.

"It was hard to get them to even tie it up at the dock," remembered Don.

Then the boat was ignored until it was time for a half-assed, rushed rehab when preparing for the next trip. Rusted and ragged she limped along her final voyage, from beginning to end.

Don put it this way, "I hadn't even thought about the boat since the end of the first trip… and that was on purpose." When the crew thought they had everything cleaned up and

fixed, they left for Nassau, only to discover the metal fuel tanks that had been sitting empty, were badly rusted, and contained so much moisture contamination in the fuel that the engine didn't want to run. "There was so much shit in the fuel that the filters couldn't keep up, we could have used 500 replacement filters," said Don.

Once again Don was the fly-in mechanic to figure out how to get the engine running acceptably. "I hooked up a 55-gallon drum on the stern as a day tank, then added as many more drums as would fit on the back of the boat to hold diesel that could be pumped into the day tank," explained Don. "It had to go about 1100 miles to Columbia, where there was bad fuel to be had also." Butch added that the fuel in Colombia was always poor quality, "usually about 10 to 20 percent water." The Sweetie Pie wound up sailing into Colombia late.

The loading went according to plan, but the trip back took 11 days. After eight days Neil, the Whalebone and the Terrapin sailboats started going out to wait for the boat. "I knew it couldn't be there yet, so all they were doing was getting the crew banged up and burned out," said Don.

"The third night when the boat finally came was really bad enough weather that we shouldn't have been out in it," Butch said. "The wind was blowing hard out of the west and it was rough." Neil was the skipper on the boat and got into really shallow water on the back side of Lower Matecumbe Key and sheared off the rudder. Butch ran forward to put out the anchor, but someone had used the line to tie up the sailboat and hadn't reattached it to the anchor, a rookie mistake, so Butch threw the anchor over to no avail. The boat did what wind-powered, and later underpowered sailboats,

have always done when a heavy wind was on them. It moved with the wind, straight toward the island. Before too long the boat was beached on the shoreline, near its lost rudder.

Dripping wet and wearing their life jackets, the two huffed it over to a "funky corner grocery store" called Angelo's to use the payphone to make urgent calls to friends and acquaintances that had a power boat, that would allow them to make the off-load. Monroe County Sheriff's Deputies were at the store and gave some long looks at the duo, but apparently decided it was not their problem, so they said nothing.

"We got a boat from a friend named Hollywood Joe, and successfully got the load to the stash house, but the whole off-load was outrageous, it was so chaotic. The captain, C.J., was yelling and screaming; erratic, disorganized and totally frantic," said Butch, "I think he about went insane and had to be hospitalized after the trip was over." He ultimately met his end by committing suicide.

Disposition is of vital importance in a captain. "It is what it is," said Butch, "you have to be cool when you are out there doing that shit."

This was the last time they used the Terrapin sailboats. "They were sneaky, but they were a pain in the ass," explained Butch. "Power boats could do the job better, in half the time."

It was also the last time they didn't have provisions for a fourth boat, or an opportunity for the first boat to make two trips. When all the off-load boats were full there were still about 20 bales that the crew cut up and threw overboard.

They all wound up on the beach behind Cheeca Lodge, a pricey resort famous for presidential visits.

Locals were calling each other to relate that pot was floating up on Cheeca Beach, free to scoop up. "A guy at a gas station told me about it the next morning," said Butch. Disposing of pot was a bad thing to have to do, "in addition to wasting profit, it just wound the cops up that much more." It was also poor form to impact the tourist's experience in the Keys, a world class resort destination. It was an action sure to generate additional heat.

From the marijuana they did off-load, Chili was convinced that Neil, the Whalebone had stolen a bale. They were numbered to prevent pilferage by the off-loaders. "I never thought he did," said Don, "things can fall over," but the Partners never worked with Neil again. Instead Butch ultimately moved into running the off-loading operation, but that's later in the story.

The Sweetie Pie was dead at the reef and had to be towed to Bimini Boatyard on the Miami River, just down from the Customs facility. "It never ran again... just sat there until it was rusted beyond repair," said Butch. It was time to start using a much better boat, built for the job; Reverend Rick's boat, the Marcia Jean – MJ for short.

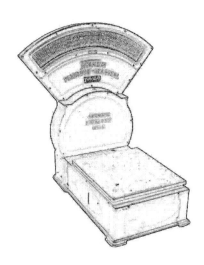

SIDEBAR 2

The Weigh-In.
All the Stars Show Up in One Place to
Divide the Spoils of a Trip.

The load was always more or less than what was agreed, but never exact. The loaders in Colombia would fill up as much as the boat would hold or as much marijuana as they had at the time. The weigh-in was when all the Partners showed up to assess what they had and divide the load, to take it to their own stash houses. Some of the other players were paid in marijuana, like Butch for his off-loading.

"Dick had a scale, so he got involved to help handle the weigh-in," said Don. The group was known for having good marijuana and some customers would pay up front to ensure their share of the load. Once, a dealer named Sal showed up at the weigh-in to which he was not invited, throwing a

briefcase with $100,000 in cash over the fence, to be first in line to buy the product. "Let us weigh it first," Don had to tell him.

After everybody got their portion at the weigh-in, they would take it back to their own stash house and prepare it for sale. The marijuana was packed in plastic garbage bags and then put in burlap, which was to provide a hand hold, so the loaders could grab it. The pot had to be stripped out of the burlap and plastic bags and sometimes there would be a few cups of seeds all accumulated in the corner or perhaps added by the Colombians.

It was then weighed on a digital scale for greater accuracy – dealers would comment if it was short – divided into forty-pound bales and wrapped in cellophane. These were then wrapped in contact shelf paper to help keep down the aroma. "We were cutting-edge for back then," said Don.

Coming up with contact paper in the quantities needed presented a problem itself. Don said he and his team bought contact paper from the Kmart in Naranja near his house. "Over the years the contact paper display got bigger and  bigger until they had a whole corner selling contact paper. At the home office of Kmart, they were probably trying to figure out why contact paper did so much better at that store than at the others in the chain," said Don. "When I

stopped they must have wondered why the bottom suddenly fell out of the contact paper market.

Scales to weigh the marijuana were another problem. "You'd go in to buy a scale from some old codger who probably sold one-a-month and it was like a police interrogation, he had so many questions for you about what you were going to do with it, and then you had to hide it at your house," said Don.

From one caper, Don accumulated 25 pounds of marijuana seeds. "That was over $8000 worth of seeds" said Don. "More importantly, it was my $8000 – I put a sprinkle here and a sprinkle there in each bag. It took more than a year to move it, but believe me, I turned those seeds into cash."

Chapter 9

A Purpose-Built Pot Smuggling Boat.
Getting All The Ducks In A Row.

Chili and Roger met Rick who had once mail-ordered "ordained minister" credentials from a place in California. After the paperwork arrived, everyone always called him Reverend Rick. He also retailed cocaine and was a pretty good customer of his own, so he used to put his stash in a safe with a time lock on it, so he couldn't get into it until "happy hour."

In 1978, Reverend Rick had completed a 48-foot boat, on a Marine Management hull. It had been started as a purpose-built vessel by other successful smugglers who never used it and sold it before it was finished. It had a 12-71 diesel engine and would make about 12 to 18 nautical miles per hour, drawing just three feet of water when empty. The Marcia Jean held 1000 gallons of diesel in its main fuel tank. They loaded about twenty 55-gallon drums of diesel onto the stern and filled large bladder tanks (one that was recycled from Don's airplane trips) that could contain another 600 gallons or more, so it could make it all the way to Colombia without the need to refuel. It could fill up there and come straight back with no need to stop anywhere. After the fuel was loaded, then the bales of marijuana were put on the boat.

There were no electronics or satellite systems, only the first-generation Loran A and a radio direction finder. There was no autopilot on the MJ. "There wasn't even a chair at the

helm at first," said Butch, "you had to stand up and drive it the entire way; on the return trip you could sit on a bale."

The crew of the MJ consisted of the captain, the mechanic and the mate. "The boat usually ran flawlessly, simple and strong with only the fuel problems from the bad diesel the Colombians always provided," said Butch. "We tried to work around the fuel problems by having a fantastic Racor fuel filter set up that allowed the mechanic to change filters while underway, so we never had to shut down the engine the whole way back," continued Butch, "that was about 250 to 300 hours."

The MJ drew such a small amount of water, she could sneak around inside passages through shallow waters in the Bahamas that most boats the MJ's size couldn't run. "They ran without lights and avoided most of the many choke points," said Butch. But even the MJ couldn't avoid the Windward Passage between Haiti and Cuba. "They tried to stay as far away from Guantanamo Bay as possible," said Don referring to the American base on the coast of Cuba.

"It [The MJ] was new, so everything worked," remarked Don, "but it was a single engine and I always thought that would someday bite our ass."

The First Trip on the Marcia Jean.
Headaches Created Multiple Off-Loading Trips.

As they were no longer using the Terrapin sailboats that also doubled as hauling containers to the stash houses, the

team needed an off-loading location to transfer the marijuana to motor vehicles, to transport it to the Redlands.

Chili and Don didn't like using rented houses, but they made this boat trip using a rented house behind the Holiday Inn in Marathon. "Rented houses always seem to have people around," explained Don, "and you had to unload 'under cover of daylight' to avoid suspicious noises and movements in the dark."

This was the first trip with Chili on-site in Colombia, securing 2000 gallons of diesel fuel, the requested 12,000 pounds of pot, and getting the boat loaded. "We always asked for 12,000 pounds and got 10 to 11,000," said Don. "Chili told me they used these giant canoes to transport everything, but I didn't picture what he meant until I saw them later."

The MJ was delayed on the way down by bad weather that caused it to be laid up in Long Island in the Bahamas for several days. It was further delayed on the way back by even worse weather.

"We used a 42-foot Chris Craft Cabin Cruiser to transport the marijuana from the MJ in the Bahamas to a house by Bonefish Towers in Marathon. They were supposed to bring half the load at a time," remembered Don, "but the Chris Craft's captain was afraid to fill up the boat, he wanted to be able to see out the windows, so he only took one-third of the marijuana."

On the trip in, the transmission blew in one of the engines, so they couldn't go back for the next load. "We had a boat with 6500 pounds of pot sitting in the Berry Islands between Bimini and Nassau," said Don.

The transmissions were counter rotating so there was a definite port and starboard side. When the replacement came in, it was the wrong side, so they had to install it backward and run the engine in reverse. While getting the second load of one-third of the marijuana, the transmission blew again and had to be replaced a second time in order to go get the balance of the product. Captain Tim had to sit on the load for three weeks while the transmission problems were repaired.

"They did such a shitty job with the off-loading, I started wanting to get a place of our own where we could control the off-loading and then were under no rush to get it up to the Redlands," explained Don.

Three Boats That Looked Just Alike.
Aqua Sport 24s Make Great Off-Loading Vessels.

After Butch experienced the fiasco with the Terrapin winding up on the beach, he was convinced that power boats were the proper way to off-load. He arranged to buy a 24-foot Aqua Sport, Family Fisherman, with twin 140 horsepower Johnson outboards and a trailer from Bob Hewes for $15,900 in cash. "A college buddy loaned me the money with the stipulation that he always got the first shot at buying my share of the load."

Getting the Aqua Sport impressed Don and soon they had three of them that looked just alike. They each had twin 140 engines and could hold 3000 pounds. "It was a nice little fleet," said Butch, "nothing flashy, just low-key, serviceable boats." The first boat went twice to bring in whatever was left after the 9000 pounds of marijuana was transported in. Drawing less than the Marine Patrol boats, the Aqua Sports were also faster.

"We never had more than one of them at the house at a time," explained Don, "so if anyone was watching, it looked like the same boat being used a lot."

The payment for the off-loaders, with their Aqua Sports was $50,000 for the Captain and boat, and $25,000 for the mate.

An Off-load House All Their Own.
The Partners Find the Perfect House to Use to Unload: Codename Oasis

Don and Chili continued not to like using a rental property as an off-load house. When they checked into renting one from another smuggler for the third boat trip, and the fee was a million dollars, Don said, "Bullshit! We'll just buy our own place."

Using their plane, he flew over the Upper Keys and Islamorada area, looking for likely prospects. "We wanted to stay in our neighborhood," said Don. "Back then they couldn't stop you until you were within the 12-mile limit of land, and I figured we could get marijuana in within that distance with no more heat than there was in the Keys at that time."

While flying, Don found a property on the ocean with its own short channel from the open water. It was for sale. Checking it out by boat, he discovered the channel had adequate depth and then by car he learned it was secluded, but right next to US 1, the Overseas Highway.

The place was for sale for $200,000, it was on five acres of undeveloped, natural property, but "none of us could qualify for a loan as we had no traceable income," explained Don. "We worked a deal to pay $125,000 down and the balance in payments." Don said that they sent "everybody out to buy cashier's checks for just under the $10,000 limit" for requiring IRS tracking paperwork – the law at the time. These were presented at the closing. "We bought it in a corporate name, back then the Feds didn't take property," explained Don.

"The place was a dump," said Don, "literally, falling down; a window fell out while we were looking at the house." It had been built for little people, "they were called midgets, back then," said Don. The counters were short, and they had these tiny toilets that you had to perch on. Yet it could be fixed up for cash and the location was perfect.

It took six months to close and get the people out because they were waiting for a new condo to be finished for them in Key Largo. "I took furniture down and stored it in the garage to give them a hint to move out, we needed them to leave because we had a load of marijuana to bring in," remarked Don. He was now officially in charge of the Oasis and the off-loading. The property became the off-load house for years and a dozen capers making two to three trips per year. They usually took August to November off during the hurricane season.

The captains with their Aqua Sports had to be trained to get into the Oasis channel at night without spotlights because there was a trailer park right next door with lots of eyes that could have seen something suspicious.

They ran aground more than once. "It was dangerous water to run aground in at night; hell, it was dangerous in the daytime," explained Don. There were shallows, a reef line and large coral heads that almost broke the surface at low tide.

The captain of the MJ met the Aqua Sports in a dark area between Hens' and Chickens' Reef, and Davis Reef, and they found each other by using the CB radios. A cousin of Don's, Scott, ran the house and used two large, "Garden Way" carts to haul the marijuana from the boat to the garage of the Oasis.

From there, with no time constraints, 1000 to 2000 pounds could be placed in each of four or five "regular pick-up trucks with grandpa-looking topper shells -- with windows so you could see in -- to transport the pot to the stash houses in the Redlands," Don related. "We put the marijuana in the bed of the truck and then some plywood and then some trash, so if anybody looked in, it looked like we were hauling trash and we only did it in the daytime, so it wouldn't look suspicious -- we used lead cars and following cars to keep an eye out for problems," explained Don. "Your brake lights could work when you started and then stop working along the way."

This was all part of the team's continuing strategy of hiding in plain sight.

A Load Is Stranded for Lack of Fuel.
The Second Trip on the Marcia Jean.

Captain Tim and his mechanic, Chris "The Wrench," made the second trip on the MJ when almost everything went

well until they were coming back and found out they had been shorted on the diesel fuel -- they ran out in the Bahamas.

We had spent years reading the Miami Herald to learn how to smuggle," said Don, "They taught me how to do it, they told me everything from early on: Where to come in, who got busted, where and how. Now with plenty of experience we could do things right, but shit like that still went wrong."

"You can't hire Harvard grads to do this job," said Butch.

Once again Don was the fly-in problem solver, called in to bring money and solutions down when the boat was out of fuel in the Berry Islands. "The boat used bladders to hold fuel," said Don, "when they were empty the crew could roll them up and hide them."

"You can't just pull into a marina to fuel up when you are carrying a load of weed," said Butch.

Don chartered a plane and flew into a resort about ten miles from where the boat was moored. He met up with the crew who came in on the Zodiac, and they all acted like he was an old friend that had come to join the party. "I had a cigar and a cocktail," related Don who visited the boat to assess the situation. On that trip, the boat was so full that the crew slept on the deck. He decided to take a 100-gallon bladder to the resort's marina to fill it up. The crew took it out to the boat and came in again hours later when different people should be around to see, if they took any notice at all. They filled the bladder a second time and 200 gallons was enough to get them the rest of the way back. Don flew back home.

"There was certainly always something that could go wrong," explained Butch, "and it always did. On the off-load, one of the Aqua Sports got out of the channel at the Oasis and ran aground, they had to back out to bring in their load."

SIDEBAR 3

John F. Was Scary Crazy.
Doing time for attempted murder, he wasn't part of the crew, but he still intimidated even from behind prison walls.

"John F. was a dangerous individual – he was a bodyguard for some notorious coke dealers who were famous in their straight jobs. Everybody was scared of John F. and we hadn't even met him – we had just heard about the things he had done," said Butch, "He let us use his place in the Redlands as a stash house while he was in jail." John F. was a friend of Roger.

Don continued, "He is only important to show you the kind of people, some of the people were. He was in jail for shooting at the Florida Power and Light guys that were working on a pole outside his house."

That was by far not his only run-in with the law.

He was once doing a marathon cocaine session with his girlfriend and his buddy, who was a Mr. Florida weightlifter or some such," said Don. They were all naked and John F. "passed out or pretended to pass out," interjected Butch.

It seems the weight lifter and the girlfriend started having sex without John F. and this didn't sit well with him.

John F. attacked the weightlifter and started beating him with a replica of a medieval mace that heretofore had been considered decorative. John F. piled the fighting weightlifter

into the trunk of his car and started down the street with the girlfriend running after him screaming.

"He was planning to take him out in the Everglades and kill him," said Butch. They were all still naked and created a disturbance that elicited a call to the authorities from the neighbors. The police arrested John F. who went to jail for the episode. "He's still out there, still alive, still living in the same house," said Don.

Prologue to Section 3:

An Enviable Record of Success.
A Custom-Designed Mother Hauling Vessel.

A purpose-built, marijuana-hauling boat with little expense spared on upgraded equipment makes multiple trips with a 90 percent success rate. Almost counts in more than horseshoes. Almost, can be a big deal in the pot smuggling business.

Section 3

Chapter 10

Butch and Otis Buy the MJ.
The Boat Would Ultimately Make More Than
20,000 Miles of Very Successful, But Not
Uneventful, Smuggling Voyages.

ISLAMORADA, Florida, with Don and Butch -- After making two trips, Reverend Rick decided he wanted to get out of the business and tried to sell his boat to the Partners. They were not interested in owning a boat, so the MJ was sold to Butch and Otis for $95,000. "I didn't really want a partner in the boat, but I was kind of coerced into it," remarked Butch.

The boat belonged to a "dummy" corporation out of Guernsey in the Channel Islands of England. The corporation had only one asset, the boat, and was called Bubbling Brook Ltd. It was legally owned by the possessor of bearer bonds. Abbey, Butch's crooked lawyer, arranged for Otis, under a fictitious name, to own the registration and the bearer bonds. No one really understood exactly how everything worked except Abbey, but when it was tested in practice, the plan did work.

"Well, now we had the MJ, with a competent crew, the Aqua Sports to off-load, with seasoned off-loaders, the Oasis to off-load and stash the weed in the Keys, vehicles to transport it, and more stash houses in the Redlands. We were

set up as a professional smuggling operation -- ready to do it properly, if not always smoothly," Butch finished.

When Butch and Otis took over the MJ, they let Captain Tim put 96-mile radar on the boat to make up for the lack of communication electronics. With this radar the captain could see all of the Bahamas, and both sides of the Windward Passage. "It was one of the best investments we made," said Butch.

"One time we had to have it worked on and when I picked up the technician at the airport he asked, 'where is your ship,' because no one put that kind of radar on a boat the size of the MJ," Butch said.

The captain of the MJ earned $75,000 for each trip and each of the two crew members were paid between $25,000 and $50,000 per trip. As owners, Butch and Otis handled paying the crew and the maintenance on the boat. It was a great relief to Don not to have to be the fly-in mechanic any more.

Don, Chili and Roger paid for the off-load crew and the marijuana from the old man and split the load with Butch and Otis. Now Don was responsible for getting the boat loaded and on its way. He also handled such things as keeping a lawyer at the ready and even having birth certificates for the crew members.

"Back then all you needed for identification to travel in the Bahamas was a birth certificate" and Don had about 20 that he had bought illegally. He also had a stack of phony Driver Licenses "but I didn't trust them as much," he said.

Butch was responsible for getting the load on the MJ to the Keys, off-loaded to the Oasis, and then up to the stash

houses in the Redlands. They used John F.'s place as a stash house and later Butch used his own and Bo's houses, which were right across the street from each other.

"We never kept weed and cash at the same house," explained Butch. "That's a rule we never broke; that way if you got busted or robbed, you wouldn't lose everything."

A primary rule of successful smuggling was to not stand out. That's why they had a transom cover made for the MJ that was the same color as the boat. Its lettering read, "Mi Tio" (My Uncle), out of Santa Marta. This was put on about 25 miles out of Colombia, so the boat appeared local in the waters off Santa Marta.

Don's job included collecting the money and paying the Colombian connection. "One time I walked into the Fontainebleau Hotel in Miami Beach with $150,000 in my boots to pay for the marijuana we had picked up in Santa Marta," remembered Don, "and another time I went into the backroom of a radio shop in deep Downtown Miami with $200,000 cash in a briefcase – that would be almost a million dollars today – I couldn't wait to get it delivered!"

In the coming years the MJ made 10 successful trips and after each one Butch bought an expensive watch, Don was still buying a case of very expensive wine.

Captain Tim ran two of the trips on the MJ for Butch and Otis, by then he had earned a pocket-full of money and was tired of the stress, so he decided to quit. "You never knew when something was going to go wrong, and he was tired of it," said Don.

Tim's mechanic, Chris "The Wrench," then captained a trip, followed by Captain Paul, then Captain Dirk, with his

nephew and an ex-Coast Guard kid for crew. Dirk ran five trips on the MJ that were successful -- but not smooth. "Nothing ever went smoothly," said Don. One problem was that, against the demands of the Partners that no cocaine be brought on the boat, the Colombians always gave the crew some for their use on the trip back. In a successful business enterprise, cocaine and marijuana smuggling don't mix.

Butch and Otis' First Trip.
Water, Water Everywhere, Especially
in the Diesel Fuel.

As good as the marijuana was that the Colombians provided, that's how bad the diesel was that they came up with. "It always had water in it," said Butch, "and that's why we had two big Racor fuel filter set ups that let the mechanic change the filter while the boat was underway. This time it was so bad that someone had to sit in the fuel compartment rotating fuel filters the entire trip, I mean steam was coming out of the breathers," said Butch. "It burned a valve that had to be repaired."

The fuel bladders were equipped with quick connects so they could burn fuel directly out of the bladder. One of them was a 500-gallon bladder, "We called them tics," said Butch. "Well one of them got loose and rolled over on Wrench pinning him beneath it right to the deck, scared the shit out of him." After that, they built wooden frames -- they called tic corrals -- to go around the bladders.

Along the way, they would throw their charts overboard after they used them so there was no record on the boat to show where they had come from.

When the off-load was completed, the crew always cleaned up the MJ, as best they could at sea and at night. They hosed off the residue and diesel smoke and headed for the Bahamas to cool off. "They went into Yacht Haven or The Poop Deck in Nassau," said Don. "They were all scammers in there," added Butch. After securing the boat, the crew flew back to Miami.

Butch and Captain Paul and their girlfriends flew over later to collect the boat and bring it back to Miami. The night they arrived they were behind Chub Cay when they decided to weigh anchor and head across the Bank toward Bimini and then across to Miami.

"People would often ask what kind of boat the MJ was, it looked like a dive boat with no dive equipment," remarked Butch. "It had air conditioning and a nice generator and the 13-foot Boston Whaler as the big dinghy. It was a nice all-around utility boat."

People in the smuggling business knew what it looked like, and that fact was brought home when suddenly they had "six or seven Cigarette boats" descending upon them that night. None of the people on the boats seemed to speak anything except Spanish. "They thought the MJ was their mother ship. 'Not us' I yelled 'You've got the wrong boat,' I kept repeating," laughed Butch.

"We brought in about 9000 to 12,000 pounds of marijuana per trip on the MJ and we tried to get good pot, we could have sold 50,000 pounds" said Butch. "The press was always about

SMUGGLERS' TIMES:
Smuggling In The Days Of Marijuana Prohibition.

right, not so compressed that it smashed the seeds and made a useless brick.

Chili had worked to get us brand new burlap coffee bags with two blue stripes and one red stripe, so it was packaged really nice and beautiful – it became our signature; of course, branding meant one bad load could make it hard for your sellers in the future."

"We were wild but not insane," stated Butch, "maybe a little stupid; I sometimes went out to the MJ to pal around with the guys, with no reason to be out there, at risk.

"Of course, once you turn the weed over into money it was a lot less scary," said Butch.

Don's Two Trips to Colombia to Load Boats.
After Five Trips Flying In, Two More
Were Enough for Everyone.

Chili or Don planned to be on hand to load every boat with 10,000 pounds of pot and 2000 gallons of diesel fuel. "Good diesel was harder to find than the pot," Don said. After Chili made three trips and his Dad made one, Don made two such trips before the communication problem caused him to quit going to Colombia.

Don stayed at the home of a prominent family. The old man was the former mayor whom they called alternately "the old man" or "the spic" depending upon whether they were talking to or about him. The old man was a big guy in stature and power, associated with the local and federal police, and the naval and marine forces. He paid everybody off, so Don was not too afraid of getting into any real trouble while he was in Colombia.

Just because he paid off the authorities didn't mean they didn't sneak around. If they could avoid an impromptu check

point, they could save the expense of that particular bribe. So, a low profile was always kept.

"When a boat went down there for a trip, we always brought the old man a case of Dom Perignon and a case of Johnnie Walker Black," said Butch.

The old man had a 20-something-year-old son who ran the marijuana business. Don stayed with them for two weeks while awaiting the boat's arrival. "There were lots of people staying there," said Don, we all ate in an open-air courtyard…lots and lots of plantains."

On the first trip, Don was surprised to see the fuel, food and the marijuana were loaded onto 50-foot long canoes that had diesel engines and a tiny cabin, to head out to find the mother boat. Don was on a "piece of shit, 21-footer with an old outboard motor." It was pitch dark and the boats couldn't find each other very easily. Their only illumination was a single light that they thought was the Santa Marta lighthouse. They didn't have any charts to see the coastline for the area.

After the loading was complete, it was about 4:00 a.m. and they pulled the canoes and the 21-foot boat up on logs on the beach where they were to meet a car nearby. Don only knew one word in Spanish besides "Cerveza" and that was because it sounded almost the same in English and that word was being shouted by men and the sound was coming from behind the other canoes.

"Policia, policia!" screamed the men as Don and his crew ran behind canoes and made for the car. "That was another time that got my attention," Don said with a laugh.

The son, named Enrique, "was a crazy Colombian kid" who knew Don as the pilot who had flown in, and wanted to

show him another airstrip. "He drove reckless and crazy, and wound up later dying in a head-on crash while passing illegally," said Don.

"We jumped into his four-wheel-drive Land Rover to set out to see this airstrip that was up in the mountains. At one point we had to get out and climb onto a tractor to cross a fast-moving little river to get to a house in the jungle," remembered Don. "It was surrounded by cages with monkeys in them and there were plenty more monkeys around the area running loose."

Don said they brought out a late lunch that he swears was monkey soup. The trip took so long they had to turn back and never made it up to see the airstrip.

The second trip to Santa Marta was much quieter, and Don even had time to take in a soccer game in the rural community.

It was decided that Don would not make any more trips to Colombia. As Chili got sick with amoebic dysentery every time he went down, and Chili's Dad was too ambitious, they hired Juan and trained him to handle the next four or five loads. "Juan wasn't bright enough to steal the connection and make it work," said Don.

Captain Markus' First Trip.
A New Captain and A Rented Sailboat
Make A Trip.

.

The methods were sound, set up and working successfully. A mother ship would bring the marijuana load

to a spot near Alligator Lighthouse and it would be off-loaded with the Aqua Sports to the Oasis and then the pick-up trucks would be used to transport the marijuana up to the Redlands' stash houses. With the machinery in place, there was every reason to schedule more trips from Colombia.

The Partners made a trip with Captain Markus, who rented a Morgan 41 out of Fort Lauderdale. The fee for the month was $10,000. This trip brought in 7000 pounds of marijuana, filling the boat up. It was on this trip that Chili's Dad met Markus.

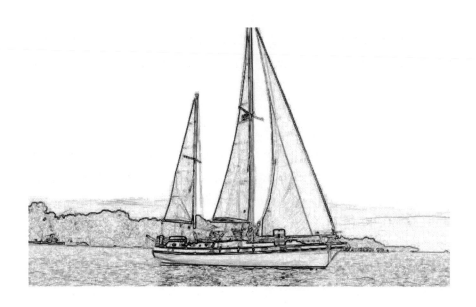

SIDEBAR 4

Chili's Dad Over-learns the Ropes of
Being a Loader.
A Key to A Successful Smuggling Enterprise Is
Working with People You Trust.

Don's smuggling scam was pretty much a family affair, using relatives and close friends he had known and trusted for many years.

As Chili or Don was on-site in Columbia for the loading of each boat, the team got burned out. In the smuggling business, getting burned out was an occupational hazard, and everyone had a life-limited career. Chili got deathly sick with amoebic dysentery on many of his trips. After two trips, the connection asked that Don not be sent back, as he didn't

SMUGGLERS' TIMES:
Smuggling In The Days Of Marijuana Prohibition.

speak Spanish and was therefore too hard to communicate with: "I didn't mind at all," said Don, "I couldn't even talk to the dog."

Chili's father, who did speak Spanish, seemed to be an excellent choice as Chili and Don's surrogate loader on-site, in Colombia and he was familiarized with the tasks and introduced to the connections. He and Chili went to Santa Marta and loaded the third trip on the MJ.

Chili's Dad worked out for the team on that trip and the next one he did solo. He learned the job and did it very well -- so well in fact, that "he stole the connection and the captain and really went solo, as he went into business for himself," said Don.

The smuggling season for the group was typically a trip before Christmas, one right after and one before hurricane season began in June. Chili had met a new captain named Markus, who had made one trip for the Partners using a rented Morgan 41-foot sailboat.

During the off-season, while the Partners were taking a break, Chili's Dad told Markus he was working for Don and Chili and arranged a trip all on his own. Captain Markus supplied a second captain and the crew, and they rented two 41-foot Morgan sailboats to make the trip. There was no wind on the trip, so the boats wound up towing each other to save fuel. They came up just south of Miami through Caesar's Creek at Elliott Key and off-loaded to shrimp trawlers which took the product to Black Point, near Homestead. "I would have never done that," said Don, "there was too much police activity going on around Black Point and a shrimp boat was too obvious as a transport vessel."

It was not until the Partners reconvened in October to get ready for a late November trip, that they found out about Chili's Dad and the free-lance trip. "They made it," said Don, so the trip was a success for Chili's Dad. There was plenty of supply and the demand was so high that it didn't really matter that he stole the business. It pissed me off because each trip burns out the captain a little bit more and we didn't make a dime off of it," explained Don, "but Chili never talked to his dad for the rest of his life."

Chapter 11

The Morgan 51 Was the First to Get Busted.
New Laws Lead to the Loss of a Load.

After the success of the first trip with Captain Markus, and a desire to control the transportation of the marijuana, the Partners decided to buy their own boat.

Don had always tried to stay away from the boats because he had so much to do in his own areas of the smuggling business. The boats were an entirely separate and great risk. Yet he and Chili decided to make an exception and invest in their own boat for the first time.

Don flew up to Wrightsville Beach and looked at a 51-foot Morgan sailboat that they bought for nearly $175,000.

Don told the captain not to sail it. "Start the engine and keep it running the whole trip," counseled Don, "that way you don't have to worry about it not starting again."

"It was a big, fat sailboat that could hold 15,000 pounds of marijuana," said Don, "all we had to do was add the fuel bladders and it was ready to go."

It was also at this time that the law about only stopping boats within the 12-mile limit changed and the Coast Guard could now stop boats in the Bahamas. Which is exactly what they did, down by Long Island. Captain Markus and the Morgan 51 became the first load the Partners lost, when they got busted one clear, sunny day. The total loss to the team was about $300,000. "It was the first one we lost," lamented Don who said he typically made about $200,000 per caper after all the expenses were paid, so the boat represented a sizeable loss.

The loss to Captain Markus was even worse; he went to jail for a year-and-a half. "We hired Anthony the lawyer for him," said Don "and we gave him money while he was in jail, for his family, and he didn't rat out anyone or anything like that, he just did his time and then retired from the business."

"We took care of his family for him," said Don, "and Chili took care of his wife, he had an affair with her while Markus was in jail, and she was hot too, like I said, Chili was big and fat, and well, kind of a pig – it's hard to imagine them together. I wouldn't even go into a convenience store with Chili and she was going to bed with him."

Chapter 12

The Boat Didn't Draw Much Water, But It Did Draw Some.
The 2nd Trip with the MJ.

Tim was captaining the MJ on the southwest side of Great Exuma, where they liked to sneak around the back side of the island and there were a couple of shallow cuts. He crossed through Jewfish Cut, around Rocky Point and on toward Brigantine Bay where he got the boat hard aground on a falling tide. They were in such shallow water that they had to off-load about 2000 pounds of marijuana to refloat the MJ.

They used the Zodiac and Boston Whaler dinghy and had to stack some of the pot on the beach of a deserted island. It took hours to complete the job and left the crew exposed during that period. But that wasn't their time to get busted.

After the off-load, one of the Aqua Sports would stay at the Oasis. The other two went to where they were typically stored. Butch and his brother Ray were at Caloosa Cove marina at about 3:00 in the morning to use their ramp, when a State Trooper stepped up with a flashlight.

"We told him we had been having engine trouble all afternoon and this was the nearest place we could get to," said Butch, "we were going to call somebody to come get us." It worked, the officer took the excuse and left without getting a good look at the Aqua Sport. "When we looked at the boat, it was covered with seeds and residue, and footprints, it was a

dirty mess," remembered Butch. All in all, it had been a lucky day in the smuggling business.

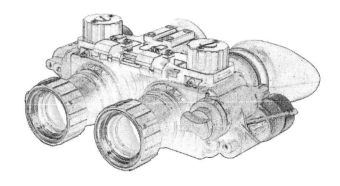

Chapter 13

Butch's Little Brother Gets To Join The Smugglers' Life.

Ray Gets An Opportunity In The Family Business As An Entry-Level Off-loader.

ISLAMORADA, Florida, with Don and Ray – Ray lost his hair as a teenager, making him, or perhaps "allowing" him to look, maybe, 10 years older than his 17 years.

He was Butch's brother, so he had an "in" with an already operational crew and he wanted to participate. Ray became an off-loader, working on the Aqua Sports with Butch and then Otis, and then Fish, unloading the MJ starting with its first voyage.

Ray worked a half-dozen trips grabbing his share of up to 80 bales and stowing them on the boat to head into the Oasis.

As a mere teenager, Ray chose to trade brawn, balls and a potential loss of liberty for a wild adrenaline rush and extremely high pay. He moved up in the business because he

chose to be paid in pot in Miami for his efforts and transported his own merchandise to the Midwest for higher returns.

"The first thing that comes to mind was those damn night vision scopes that we used," said Ray. "I remember zeroing in on the MJ the first time and I thought, damn, this thing is like magic. But they were a double-edged sword. You used them with one eye, so I had to take my glasses off and I didn't have contacts, well I can't see shit without my glasses."

Ray continued, "With the scope you could see in the dark, but it'd fuck up your vision in that eye. If you look through it for two minutes, then your vision is screwed for two minutes. It was dark as shit out there, we needed something. But if you hit a light, like when you are coming back to shore, it messes you up something fierce."

"The second thing that I will remember for my whole life is how scared I was when I ran us aground." Ray said, "I was a kid right out of high school, barely turned 18, if I had, by that time. There were bales stacked all over, loading down the Aqua Sport. Some of them were double bales that weighed 80 pounds. I was sitting on the bales navigating and the windshield that is usually shoulder high, well I was two feet above it from being boosted up on the bales."

Ray said that the engines would come out of the water when the heavy boat would rock, and you could hear the sound of the propellers as each, in turn, came out of the water and cavitated. "Blub, blub, blub," he mimicked.

"At slow speeds the Aqua Sports were tippy," said Don. "They have high sides and with 3000 pounds of marijuana on them they would rock and roll." Don said that other boats

were better for carrying a big load, "T-Crafts," for example, were wider with a flat bottom.

"They would kill you if you were in any kind of seas, but you could stack a lot of pot on them," said Don. "Lobster fishermen used them for their traps. They developed a reputation as a great off-load boat, so we didn't want them. We used the family fisherman, so it looked like a leisure boat, it wasn't suspicious-looking that the boat might have had a business use."

Ray said "It was a great boat that held a bunch of weed, the worst part about it was getting the bales unloaded from the cuddy cabin. You could barely get a bale through the opening. Especially the double bales that were 80 pounds. They were about three-and-a-half feet long, so you couldn't grab them, you had to wrap your arms around the middle and kind of hug them."

"Then it was a bitch to clean it up later," said Ray, "because every nook and cranny would have residue or some stems and seeds in it. I was just thinking today how great a cordless vacuum cleaner would have been."

"We could have used Clorox to clean the residue," said Don, "But none of us ever thought of it back then."

"I was navigating, excited to be in the smuggling business, even if it was a low rung on the ladder and we were just inching along, using the scope, heading into the Oasis and I was just out of the channel by a few yards. It was an unforgiving channel because it had been dug by a crane, years before, so it went straight down and straight up, shallow enough to stand next to it," said Ray.

"Suddenly I hear this horrendous noise and I'd run us up on the rocks" said Ray, "I was so scared I'd fucked up big time and I thought Butch was going to kill me."

If the boat had been going faster, it would have probably knocked a hole in it. But, they were able to back out and get into the channel and continue the off-load.

"There was nothing like being a kid and seeing that mother boat, with all those guys waiting to unload." Ray had been on the first Aqua Sport, so he always made two trips to the MJ. "I remember one time, being at the boat and the other Aqua Sport was still there. We were on each side of the boat, unloading. It was a sight."

Another visual Ray remembers from that time is coming into the Oasis and seeing the guys with their big garden carts waiting to unload the bales and carry them into the four-car garage. "It was an awesome sight, we were there for a minute, so we got to see a little bit of what they had going on."

"I could see some of the crews' vehicles hidden among the wooded acres. Thinking about the next few hours, running on maximum adrenaline. I would get the biggest rush I've ever had," Ray said.

"It's hard to describe, but there is nothing really, quite like being 18 years old and looking through that night scope and seeing that boat there, with those dudes sitting there, with all those bales stacked up waiting to off-load," remembered Ray, who said he is working on a screenplay about his adventures and likes to think in terms of visuals. "They were ready to go. It was surrealistic, to say the least, there was lots of surreal shit out there."

In the shadows of the off-load Ray could see the boys doing their jobs quickly, "we were ready to go get the second load, people were on their way in. We would soon put it in trucks to take it up to the stash house. There was no fucking around. It was a goddamned machine running smoothly, like clockwork."

Ray used to keep his personal boat at Clark's Marina which is where Worldwide Sportsman is today. Butch had lived on his Chinese Junk in the basin behind it. Ray used to hang out at the marina and would sometimes smoke weed with Fish. He is the one that recruited Fish to be a captain on the off-loads.

Fish was as salty as anyone I ever met," said Ray, 'he lived on an old sailboat with an old, old pit bull. "He was gruff, and he didn't say a lot. He was not a dumbass, just disheveled and rough. He'd seen everything and nothing much phased him. He knew a little about what we were doing. Well, he never had a nickel. I always had weed. I was just a kid that smuggled pot and had money, hanging out down there. I got approval from the Partners and asked him to work with us. He lit up like a Christmas tree; you'd think he won the lottery."

Of course, Fish was a sailor, he wasn't an outboard man. We had to teach him to operate the Aqua Sport and navigate the waters at night without any lights.

Fish was cool, but this was new for him. He was nervous on the first gig. He had his asshole pinched up pretty tightly that night. I had to calm my captain down, but once we got rolling he was a natural at it.

After my first load, I enjoyed it. Of course, it was scary --
but exciting as shit," said Ray, "I got into it, got into the boat
part of it. I loved it," said Ray. "My biggest fear was later
when I got in the truck to take off out of there with a load of
pot. If I remember correctly we had somebody watching the
road. And when we moved up the road to the stash house, we
had other cars on the highway in front of and behind us."

Don monitored the off-load activity by scanner and radio
from a house nearby. "We called it the command post. I could
see the gate to watch if there was anything going on at the
drive into the Oasis." Until Don told him about his proximity
to the action, Ray had never known he had been around.

Ray explained that "One Aqua Sport "lived" at the Oasis,
one was docked behind Otis' house on Lower Matecumbe
and the third was put back on a trailer and kept parked in
somebody's yard. One night they couldn't raise the guy with
the trailer on the radio, so they pulled in Caloosa Cove
Marina to use the pay phone. Communicating was always a
problem."

The episode represents a unique opportunity to hear the
same story from both Butch and Ray's point of view.

"It was about four o'clock in the morning and we pulled
up to the dock after a successful off-load," remembered Ray.
"We'd done a quick job cleaning the boat, but maybe too
quick. We had some rods on the boat as props, but we didn't
look like we had been fishing, I'll put it that way, there were
no fish guts or anything. We came up to the dock and a cop
steps out to take the line. 'I got you,' he said, and I wasn't
exactly sure if he meant he was taking the line or that he was

busting us. My stomach felt sick. We were off-guard, not expecting to meet anyone at that time of the morning."

Ray continued that Butch told the guy a story that was not too good, about how they had engine trouble, and this was where they were just now getting to and were to call someone to meet them to pick them up.

"While we are talking, every time I looked anywhere I could see residue," said Ray. "The cop had a flashlight and he talked to us for what seemed like an eternity, but he bought Butch's story and didn't look too closely. We made a phone call and hightailed it the hell out of there as quickly as we could."

Except for that incident and running the boat aground, Ray remembers the off-loading episodes as being "a euphoric almost high-fiving, action-packed, kind of thing. Just rolling in and rolling out with everyone doing their job." Well, maybe there was one more to add to the incidents.

"It was my very first trip. We pulled up next to the boat and I was getting ready to grab the side to tie off and the crew member on the MJ hit me square in the face with an 80-pound double bale. It knocked me down, broke my nose and destroyed my glasses. "I got injured on the first second of the first minute of my first gig," said Ray. "It really rattled my cage. I remember trying to piece my glasses back together on our way back in because I needed to see to help navigate the Aqua Sport in. "I gave the guy some shit about it, I said 'Jesus Christ dude, relax.'"

"I was pretty much thrown into the fire to learn as I went along," said Ray. "I knew where to show up and when and that was really it. I knew about an inch worth of a mile of

planning. I rode the boat in and out of the Oasis, loaded and unloaded bales, spent about an hour-and-a-half to clean up the boat, and then got it back where it belonged. And they gave me a bunch of money for the long night's work. It was a life-changing experience. It was such a rush, because I was a kid."

To celebrate Ray's birthday, they had a party that Chili and Roger attended. Chili had brought a bottle of Chateau Lafitte Rothschild vintage 1959 and Ray commented that the bottle was from the year he was born. This was when Chili and Roger found out about Ray's young age. Don wasn't at the party and he didn't know Ray other than his name.

Chili went ballistic complaining to Butch, "What do you mean bringing a kid that young on a caper?" he exclaimed. "But we had been doing it and I was successful," Ray said.

Ray also worked driving a truck up to the Redlands stash house, transporting the inventory for the weigh-in. He got paid in pot, so his share was loaded into big Ford LTDs and Chrysler Imperials, with huge trunks to take it to Indiana for retailing.

Chapter 14

*You Drive Differently When You
Are Carrying A Load.*
Transporting 1000-Pounds of Marijuana by Pickup
Truck to the Redland's Stash House.

"I'm not an easily scared guy and I sure wasn't back then," remembered Ray, "but there was always heat on the road no matter who we had driving in front of us or behind us. It seemed like anytime I pulled out of the Oasis a sheriff's car would pull up right behind me and then you kept passing them heading south as we were heading up, out of the Keys. I've seen them parked on the side of the road and it was in my imagination, or the adrenaline or the fight-or-flight response, but in my mind, I knew it had something to do with me."

"It could have had something to do with the fact I hadn't slept very much in the past two days. After we got the boats and everything all stowed from the off-load, we would try to

grab a few hours of sleep until the sun was up the next morning," said Ray, "Then we drove the trucks up to the stash house."

Don added, "We didn't want to arouse suspicions by having pickup trucks on the road in the wee hours of the morning heading north."

Ray said, "As I drove up US 1, I felt like we stuck out like a sore thumb. With the boats I felt like I could have escaped. I could have jumped into the water in the dark and swam to shore if I needed to, but when you're on the road it's like a funnel. There's no place to hide."

It was probably appropriate that Ray felt this way on his first trip when, "I had a 1975 Chevy 4-wheel drive with monster mud tires and a topper."

Don said they only used that truck that one time because we were short on vehicles. "I got another vehicle as soon as I could," said Ray. We typically drove nice Chevy pickup trucks with a topper on them. It was a grandpa-looking truck that wasn't conspicuous.

After I got off the 18-mile stretch and headed into the Redlands where I pretty much blended in," remarked Ray, "I would relax a little bit."

Ray didn't usually go to the same stash house twice. Roger arranged for a lot of different houses in the Redlands. "I usually had a map with me," he said, "This was before GPS." He would go to a house he had never been to before where there were people that he didn't know. "I had a high trust level -- and hope level -- back then," Ray remembered. "Later we took everything to Butch or Bo's houses."

"Sometimes we had the drivers leave the truck in a mall parking lot and someone else picked it up and took it to the stash house, then brought it back later when it was empty," related Don.

"We had buyers from New York and New Jersey that would do the same thing in reverse. They would leave their car in a parking lot," explained Don. "We'd have it picked up and then leave it with the load in it in the parking lot again, for them to come and retrieve."

At the weigh-in they would split up the load. "Butch and Otis and I got paid in pot. Butch took his to different cities in Indiana and Otis and I partnered up and took it to Bloomington. We could fit 300 pounds in the trunk of a big four-door sedan," said Ray.

"Otis and I would take turns driving and sleeping in the backseat. We always had a spare tire behind the driver's seat with luggage stacked over it," Ray remembered. "We wore out a few sedans."

As law enforcement got wise to the scams, transporters started getting busted. "We decided we fit the profile: Some young guy in his twenties driving a Ford LTD Brougham. There couldn't be that many kids driving their grandmother's car. So, we swapped to other cars," Ray said.

Used cars drew less attention. Butch had one that was a pale blue Plymouth Fury that was the same kind of car that municipalities had and that were also unmarked police cars.

"You pulled up some place in that and it looked like a detective. More than once, he showed up unannounced at someone's house and they thought the heat was on them," said Ray.

"The best car I ever had for transporting was a 1978 Subaru GL 4-door. This was when I went into business by myself taking it to Indiana. It was a little bitty car, like a tiny square Honda, but it had an enormous trunk. The spare tire was a donut and it was mounted under the hood over the engine, so that made even more space," Ray said, "It held nearly 300 pounds. Nobody suspected a vehicle like that was smuggling. I didn't fit anybody's profile driving that thing."

As I moved up and made more money -- got higher up into smuggling -- I always felt that my brother tried to keep me down as just hired labor. He was less and less comfortable with me working in the business. Part of it could have been that he was being a bit over-protective as an older brother, Chili was over-protective like that and seemed to worry about me because I was much younger than everyone else, but I think part of it was sibling rivalry."

Ray said, "I remember being about 20 and taking my Subaru and $25,000 worth of pot and coming back with a briefcase with $100,000 and I'd go back and do it again, until I owned all the money in that case.

Of course, after Butch bought the MJ they tightened up wild behaviors of all the workers running amok. Especially, a guy like me who was young and had money hanging out like a madman at the Tiki bar. So, I understand there were some concerns on the bosses' part.

I fucked up on several occasions as a kid, but in business I never messed up. I never got busted or got anybody in trouble, but I enjoyed my leisure time and I had a lot of money. That could be a problem, of looking like too much of a big shot in a very small place.

Don said that was why he hired workers from other areas than the Keys that weren't so flamboyant. Of course, "There was Chili and Roger, the two wildest people I ever met, and they were my partners."

Ray admitted that "some of the wildest times of his life happened before he was 21. I'd give anything to go back there right now -- the risk and the whole deal – I'd do it all over again in a second."

Chapter 15

Ray Gets Involved With "Imperial Entanglements."
He Was Calm Because He Thought
He Was Already Busted.

"It was in 1979, I was cruising along I-75 in north Florida in my little Subaru, the air shocks pumped up and the car loaded to the gills with 280 pounds of pot. The trunk would barely close. I was listening to the World Series on the radio. My suitcase was in the back and an itty-bitty-ass TV because my buddy that I would be staying with in Indiana didn't have a TV in the guest room," remembered Ray.

"Well I see this poor guy pulled over with a State Trooper vehicle in front of him and another behind him and an unmarked Ford LTD in front of the first Trooper's car. They had his trunk open and I think 'poor bastard' as I drive past exactly at the speed limit trying to look innocent."

"All three of them turn and put their eyes right on me. The suspect may have even stared at me. I became their focus and it was not just my imagination that time at all."

Ray continued driving and took a deep breath of relief moments later when he crossed the state line into Georgia. About two miles in, he sees the blue lights in his rearview mirror where they had followed him across state lines.

"I think, 'Shit, I'm done,' because they followed me across state lines and next I was in the same position as the poor bastard, except the unmarked car pulled in behind the Trooper's vehicle. The Trooper behind me gets out of his car and comes up and asks me for my driver's license and I comply while asking him politely and respectfully, but mostly respectfully, what this is about?"

The State Trooper says they are pulling over several different people tonight because there was a guy out there selling stolen electronics on the CB and they noticed Ray had a CB antenna on the roof which he did and which everybody did back then. The Law Enforcement official asks Ray to step out of the car.

Ray is sure that a request to open the trunk is the next question. "Don't ask me how -- it was a gift from God because I was already seeing myself imprisoned at Eglin Air Force Base – but my whole body went into a state of calm and I leaned up against his car and I was talking to him as though I didn't have a trunk-load of weed," said Ray.

"They were shining a flash light into the Subaru and the plain-clothes guy said, 'I noticed you've got a TV back there' and I said to look at it, that is an old worn out TV, it doesn't look like stolen electronics does it?"

They asked Ray what he was doing, and he responded that he was going to visit his mother and she didn't have a TV in the guest bedroom. The secret to a good lie is to keep it close to the truth. "I'm transporting $100,000 worth of weed," versus "I'm going to visit Mom." The TV in the spare room was the same either way. "If they had had dogs, I would have been caught. The Subaru and I prevailed. I ran the wheels off the little car and I tried to find another one and never could replace it."

Five minutes later the cop comes up and says that they are sorry to have bothered Ray. He says to have a good evening and be careful on the trip.

I was never so happy in my life not to have heard three words. "Pop the trunk."

"I was in disbelief as I got back in my car and started up," said Ray. The two State Troopers left and drove across the median and headed south, but the unmarked car just sat there.

Ray said "I took off and, you know how you take off after you just got pulled over -- real fucking careful – real gently, driving straight within the lines, and this guy got behind me, a quarter mile or so back. He's there and he keeps following me and I thought "Well, you're in this big-ass gas guzzler and I'm in this little Subaru and I just gassed up. I will run your ass out of gas because there's no way I'm pulling off at an exit ramp or stopping at a gas station or at a rest area to puke and cry, or just collapse.

"I didn't have that luxury because this mother fucker was following me. I got 35 or 40 miles up the road and I saw him finally pull off. I went another 20 miles or so and then I pulled off to regroup. I remember we had pagers back then,

because I got a hold of my buddy up in Indiana and I said, "Dude, I've got some bad news for you: the price of this weed just went up!"

SIDEBAR 5

The Smugglers' Highway.
The Team's Preferred Route for a Laden Ship
from Colombia to Islamorada.

ISLAMORADA, Florida, with Don and Butch -- It was a "pleasure cruise" on the way down, making stops along the way. Once the boat was loaded and they left Colombia, the next few days were possibly the most stressful of their lives and the fact that Enrique insisted upon slipping the crew some cocaine for use on the trip didn't help their clear thinking and disposition for the 1150-mile trip, at about seven miles per hour, from Santa Marta to just offshore from the Oasis.

The first part of the trip was a 425-mile leg of open water to the Southeast tip of Haiti on a compass setting of 330 degrees. The trade winds ran 15 to 25 miles per hour for the entire way. This heading took them through a 150-mile run in the southern part of the Windward Passage that brought them up to the lower Bahamas' island of Great Inagua. After rounding the southern tip of Haiti, they stayed in Haitian waters because that country didn't have any real law enforcement out there, just some junk boats that rarely ever went out. At the northern tip of Haiti there were about 70 more miles of open water into the islands in the Bahamas chain.

The Bahamian Defense Force had a little base on the southernmost island of Great Inagua where there was a police presence. At that time a lot of fishermen out of Cuba

would come into that bank in Bahamian waters and the Bahamians were beginning to protect their fisheries. "So, there was heat in the area," said Butch, "but we never did have any trouble with them."

After getting into the Bahamas chain the crew had reached a milestone and started feeling a bit better, because they were out of the Windward Passage and past Guantanamo Bay, where there were big U.S. Coast Guard and Navy bases. There was always heat near there but that was clear across the Windward Passage on the western side, on the east end of Cuba.

Now the MJ was in the shallow reef-strewn waters of the Bahamas, where the boat was at her best. Staying in these areas, where there were very few tourists, and only a few Bahamian fishermen's boats, the MJ was relatively clear of law enforcement.

It was a 145-mile trip up to the south point of Long Island, which they passed on the west, staying clear of the deep-water channels where the law enforcement boats could go. Then they would slip between the Jumentos and Long Island, and head for the southern Exumas. They were over half-way home by then.

In these waters the only charts available were unreliable British Admiralty "works of art" with soundings made in the eighteenth century. The area was so filled with coral heads and reefs that they had to time it to go through there when it was daylight. "It was truly excellent, seat-of-the-pants seamanship, it was eyeball navigating," remembered Butch.

They worked their way through the western side of the Exumas, up to Channel Cay, "which is where they did all

their good sneaking around," said Butch. Then it was north to Hog Cay Cut where they got into beautiful clear, sheltered water and calm seas for about 70 miles.

Rocky Point was a reef that did have a lighthouse and there were usually some boats anchored around there. "It was a good spot to take a little break, spear some fish, collect some conch and plan out the rest of the trip so they got to the Keys at about 10:00 at night," said Butch.

Rocky Point is also where Tim captained them into the mess where they had to off-load pot onto the beach to re-float the boat. From the west side of Rocky Point to the north end of Andros and the Jolters where they crossed onto the Bahamas Bank was 170 miles of water that was 10 to 12 feet deep. Usually lightly traveled, it was a nice trip.

They went through an open channel between the north end of Andros at Nicholls Town and Man of War Cay, and Nassau, then picked their way through the reef in daylight at Jolter Cay. Very few people went through there because 20 miles north was the Northwest Channel that was a well-marked and lit choke point that the crew avoided. "Part of the smuggling deal was taking the sneaky way but getting through the Jolters, you had to have good daylight to do that," said Butch.

After they made their way through the reef, they could make their way across the Great Bahama Bank, heading toward Bimini where there were a couple of choke points near Gunn Cay and Cat Island cuts. They were about 60 miles from the Gulfstream. At this point they were in the home stretch, only about 140 miles from the off-load spot, so speed and timing were critical. From South Riding Rock near

Bimini to the Oasis off-load point was 78 miles of open ocean.

The MJ headed toward a dark point between Hens' and Chickens' Reef, and Davis Reef. They would communicate with the Aqua Sports using the CB radios and the off-load boats would get on the reverse or reciprocal compass heading and they would soon see each other and begin the off-load without the MJ ever stopping.

About 2000 pounds of marijuana would be put on each boat, with the first one coming back to make the fourth trip, if needed. This was about 40 or more of the nearly 50-pound bales, wrapped in burlap.

Chapter 16

Even Successful Trips Are Never Completely Smooth.
It Was Getting Too Hot in The Cabin.

The Wrench was the captain of the MJ on this trip and they were between Colombia and Cuba, when all hell rained down on them. The 13-foot Whaler dinghy was on the roof of the cabin where it always nested, secured by cables and chains.

As they were underway, they suddenly noticed liquid fire running down the railings and bouncing into the water. It was flaming fiberglass falling down from the dinghy which was well on fire. Apparently, a battery had turned over and a spark had ignited some of the fuel from the six, six-gallon tanks. They used bolt cutters and got the boat off the MJ and cut it loose in the ocean.

It could have been much worse if they hadn't noticed the fire when they did, "but it was a pretty decent adventure for the day," remarked Butch.

The Coast Guard contacted them about a year later. They had found the boat floating. It had burned to the waterline, and they wanted to know what happened. The advertising used to boast that Boston Whalers were unsinkable, and it was apparently true.

Tight Connections for a Fuel Injector Pump.
The 4th Trip with the MJ.

Paul was captaining for the one and only time the MJ was dead in the water needing a repair, in Colombia. On the way down, they were noticing that the fuel injector pump was going out. By this trip the boat had been equipped with a Ham radio and they got a message to Butch about the problem.

Friday afternoon found Butch at his home in the Redlands calling around looking for the replacement. He found one in West Palm Beach at a store that opened at noon on Saturday. "I had to get the part to Downtown Miami (about 80 miles) to the electronics store by 1:00 pm so the guy could catch a plane from Miami to Cartagena to get it to Santa Marta to meet the boat," explained Butch.

"I drove like a maniac with my flashers on and my car alarm blaring, driving about 95 miles per hour, but I got the part and delivered it and the guy made the flight and they received the part and got it on, and the MJ left that night coming back," remembered Butch, taking a breath.

"It was possibly the most stressful day I ever had with the whole deal, because of the driving like an insane person and the deadline, but we made it," said Butch.

Another addition to the smuggling enterprise was a bit of counterintelligence activity in the form of radio scanners at the Oasis. Don had purchased, "For a thousand dollars, I remember that," the secret radio frequencies used by the Marine Patrol, Sheriff's Office and U.S. Customs, so the team could monitor what was going on when a load was coming in. Besides that, Don also kept the scanners on all night, every

night with a voice activated recorder. Then each morning, he could listen to a tape of what happened overnight. "There were lots of other people running scams and lots of other loads not getting in," he said. "It was a pretty nifty set up," added Butch.

This was also the trip where they experimented with a new product and threw about 200 pounds of hash on the boat, to see how it went over in the South Florida market. "It was terrible hash," said Don. "I kept it in my attic for a fucking year and finally had to sell it dirt cheap just to get rid of it."

Bad Weather Forces a Cruise Through *Nassau Harbor.* A Full Load And Congestion On The 5th Trip with the MJ.

Weather issues affected all the trips, but none so much as when Captain Dirk was forced to go outside, on the east side of the Bahamas chain and cross through Nassau Harbor, carrying about 10,000 pounds of marijuana.

"The weather must have kept the smell from being noticed," said Butch, "you could smell the burlap a mile downwind." The weather and luck must have been what kept them from being stopped, because there were few spots that had more eyes and potential heat than Nassau Harbor. "But the weather gave them no choice," said Don.

There Were No Antibiotic Drugs.
Earaches In The Middle of the Caribbean,
On Trip Six.

There are tradeoffs for a big boat that draws very little water, and that comes in the steering. The MJ had a wide beam, a flat bottom with a tunnel drive and a low profile of about 15 feet, plus it only drew about three-feet empty, four-feet with a load, so it could go inside the Bahamas chain and pick its way along in shallow water that is about four- to five-feet deep.

The Bahamian Defense Force was using World War II-era boats that were like miniature ships. They drew about 10-feet of water, so BDF boats were not even running in the same areas where they could see, much less stop the MJ.

The down side to the MJ was that, with no keel, it was not an easy boat to steer. Once they made it through the Windward Passage there were lots of trade winds and currents to contend with. "You had to steer it the entire way, so it was a tiring boat to pilot," said Butch.

A Wagner auto pilot that had been made for Pacific fishing boats had been installed and that made a big difference. Loran C and a radio directional finder had also been added so the boat could follow a straight line all the way to their favorite AM radio station, WQAM Miami.

A trip down to Colombia was, in theory, a relaxing pleasure cruise. "They were not doing anything illegal and made stops along the way," said Don. "In fact we had a hard time kicking them off the dock to get on with the trip."

The crew did pull into resorts and marinas and tip the kids there big, to do simple chores. Butch said, "Bahamian Kids did so well from us and others in the smuggling business, as time went by you couldn't even hire them to clean the boat."

Getting rope wrapped around the prop is an all too common occurrence in the ocean and that's what caused Captain Dirk to be diving in the midst of a trip down to Colombia. But this time it caused him to get an ear infection that wouldn't clear up. Ultimately, it got bad enough that he had to dock the boat and fly back to Miami to see a doctor and get some antibiotics before he could continue the trip.

A Crew Member Is Lost At Sea.
The 7th Trip with the MJ.

Captain Dirk always used an ex-Coast Guard kid, named Theo, as the mate on his trips, even after he was lost at sea.

On the way to Colombia, when it was just three guys on a pleasure cruise, they always sailed to Nassau first and checked it with the authorities to get clearance to sail

Bahamian waters for six months. They would, of course, not "check out" when they headed to Colombia and back. Then after the trip north, they darted in on an overnight trip to the Keys and back to Bahamian waters as though they have been cruising the island chain the entire time.

The seventh trip had gone smoothly, too smoothly because something could always happen. The MJ had successfully off-loaded and was headed back across the Gulfstream to the Bahamas when the weather kicked up a bit. "The ex-Coast Guard Kid was fucking around tying on this eight-foot dinghy when a wave knocked him and the dinghy overboard," said Butch. "Nobody noticed for a bit, long enough that they couldn't find him." Theo was lost at sea.

"They had something like seven planes looking for him," remembered Butch, "but no one could find hide nor hair of him and after a couple of days it was decided that he was just lost."

"We had kind of written him off," said Butch. Then on the third day, Butch got a collect call from Bimini. "Theo said, 'yeah, I drifted into Bimini.' He had actually sailed himself over there with his foul weather gear and an oar," related Butch. "He was a badass, I'll tell you, because I thought for sure he was dead."

Theo made it into the dinghy and had wound up on Bimini; safe, sunburned and thirsty. He was ready for the next trip on the MJ.

What Is Remembered About a Successful Trip.
The 8th Trip with the MJ.

Don reached into his Cadillac, parked in front of the liquor store and popped the trunk, as the young man pushed a hand truck with three cases of wine toward the back of the car. Don reached into his pocket for a hefty tip while the young man loaded several cases of Chateau Lafitte Rothschild, 1970 vintage, into the trunk and closed the lid.

~

Butch sat a watch case on the dresser and opened the top drawer. He took off the watch he was wearing and placed it into its own watch case from amongst the dozen or so in the drawer. Next, he opened the new watch case, removed the Rolex and placed it on his wrist. He put the now empty, new watch case into the drawer and closed it.

~

Chili sat on the couch, pipe in hand as his wife bitched about something he didn't bother to hear, then she sat down next to him and took the pipe for her own use. He always admitted he had a drug problem: it was his wife.

~

Roger played pool louder than possibly anyone on the planet, or at least at the Ocean View. That night he played pool, very loudly, as he ran up a huge tab for everyone at the O.V.

~

Otis opened the colorful wooden box and removed the Cuban Monte Cristo. He unwrapped the cellophane sheath, and licked the length of the cigar. Then he cut the tip and lit it with a satisfied smile.

~

Chapter 17

Boarded by The Bahamian Defense Force.
The 9th Trip with the MJ.

After a successful off-load, Captain Dirk and his crew headed back to Orange Cay in the Bahamas, cleaning up along the way. Early the next morning they were boarded by the Bahamian Defense Force who found some residue and arrested them, impounding the boat.

"It was one scary episode," said Butch, "very much not cool." They tried to beat confessions out of the crew using rubber hoses, but nobody talked. The crew's only identification was the bogus birth certificates for each of them. They used these to get released on bail, which they jumped, under assumed names. Anthony the lawyer got the boat back because it was registered to the offshore corporation. The legal fees to get the boat returned only came to $100,000, just a bit more than the replacement value of the MJ.

The crew was jailed in "Fox Hill Prison, which is no day at the beach," said Butch. The "notorious Caribbean prison is something from centuries past, with buckets instead of plumbing and scant electricity. It catered to a really rough crowd. It was a bad place for three white American boys."

Anthony was able to get the crew off and the boat returned due to a bribery deal. "It was all under the table to the right people," said Don.

That was the last trip on the MJ. The boat had a distinctive profile and "the heat was on the boat," said Butch, "it was on a hot sheet somewhere." No one even wanted to bring it back to Florida, so Butch brought the MJ over so it could be sold. "Some other smugglers got it and got busted on their first trip." he said.

The team took about six months off to let things settle down a bit and then regrouped to assess where to go next.

SIDEBAR 6

Don is Enlisted to Search for a Downed Pilot.
Friends Ask Don to Fly to Andros Island, Looking
For Signs of an Overdue Plane.

Six-hundred-and-twenty-five Loadstar aircraft were built by Lockheed starting in 1939, to use during World War II. They had two big, powerful radial engines that were unreliable from the factory and one of these worn-out beasts had made its way to Red-Headed Chuck.

"I told him I wouldn't taxi around the airport in it, much less fly anyplace," remembered Don. "And I said he shouldn't either, but he did. He made a run in it."

One morning Don received a call from Red-Headed Chuck's girlfriend. It seemed Chuck was overdue and had never showed for a rendezvous at Billy Island, a little Key near Andros Island used by many smugglers. No one had heard from him. So, Don and Butch snuck over to have a

SMUGGLERS' TIMES:
Smuggling In The Days Of Marijuana Prohibition.

look. "I knew how to get to the Bahamas without anybody knowing," said Don.

The island had a pot-holed airstrip of sorts that ended at the beach. Boats could pull up on the sand and off-load 50 feet away. The airstrip was flanked by 55-gallon fuel drums and smudge pots and had a DC3 parked at the far end. Other than that, the place seemed deserted.

Don flew low and slow, the length of the runway, about 10 feet off the ground and asked Butch to look out and tell him how the airstrip looked. "It was a dangerous runway and the landing looked hairy," said Butch "and it was."

There was no one around, but all kinds of footprints and debris showing that plenty of rushed activity had been there. The DC3 turned out to have been gutted. "It was never going to fly again," Don remembered.

As they flew out and got a few miles away, a Coast Guard plane flew over. That could have resulted in some awkward questions or some trouble about their presence on the island. Butch said, "That was an adventure!"

"The whole place was really kind of creepy," said Butch. "There were about eight or 10 planes crashed in the water around the airstrip but none of them were big enough for a Loadstar," said Don. They never found any sign of him or his plane.

"Between Haiti and Colombia, the water is thousands of feet deep," explained Butch. That was part of the risk to life and liberty. "It was not just fun and games, it was some serious shit," Butch said.

No one ever heard anything from Red-Headed Chuck again. He was just lost. He was dead. As Vonnegut said, "And so it goes."

Chapter 18

The Big Meeting.
The Partners, and Butch and Otis Meet to
Map Out Multi-Million Dollar Deals.

Like in any enterprise, organizational, planning and marketing meetings need to be held to map out methods and operations. The smuggling business is no different except that the decorum is considerably more casual, although the Partners had agreed along about the fourth trip on the MJ that cocaine use was prohibited at business meetings.

So, the group of Don, Roger, Butch and Otis was taken aback by Chili's disheveled appearance when he wandered in, a free-base cocaine pipe and torch in hand.

"After a big loss due to the MJ and its crew being taken, we were meeting to discuss multi-million dollar scams that would go on for years and Chili comes in with a pipe," remembered Don. "It wasn't crack, because that shit hadn't been invented yet, but he was free-basing and adamant that we should all try it," said Butch. "I said, 'absolutely not, I don't need another bad habit' and we all said no."

That's when I said, "I quit!" stated Don. "And to my surprise, Roger said 'I quit,' too," although both still invested in deals.

Don remembered "I told him: 'I'm quitting because I don't want a partner to die in the middle of a scam, and me not know what's going on.'"

"When Chili walked in with the pipe, that was probably the craziest thing he ever did," said Butch. "It was the beginning of the end for him."

Don remembered, "One of my thoughts was that we'd been losing money and I thought that I'd rather spend it than lose it."

So, it was decided that Chili, Otis and Butch would work together. They would pay Don to use the Oasis for the off-loading and life would go on. The new team started looking for a new boat to make the Colombia to Islamorada trips.

Prologue to Section 4:

The Kind of Bird That Lays the Golden Egg:
It Might Well Be the Golden Eagle.

After Don retired the first time, Butch and Otis moved into a position as partners with Chili on The Golden Eagle. It was a caper that was planned out to make each one of them a millionaire. Also, like eggs, the best laid plans may have a few cracks in them and are apt to wind up scrambled.

Section 4

Chapter 19

Don Retires for the First Time.
Like Many Retirees, Don was Concerned about Outliving His Assets.

ISLAMORADA, Florida, with Don and Butch -- When Don quit the Partners he thought he had enough money to last him for the rest of his life. If he had that much all together after he made his first flight, it might well have been enough to tide him over for that long, but in the ensuing years he had become too accustomed to living, very well. Don drove Cadillacs, lived in multiple houses, drank expensive wines, had lavish dinners out with multiple guests, had boats and women and planes. He lived his life by the motto: "if it flies, floats or fucks – rent it." Even so, he had acquired lots of assets, including real estate and a live-in girlfriend with several needy adult kids. In short, Don had become quite accustomed to living very, very well.

After a time, Don became concerned that his burn rate meant he would run out of money in a few years. "I looked at my monthly expenses and they were over $10,000 per month – back then!" said Don, and that didn't include vacations and playing."

In order to keep up his style of living, Don decided he needed to go back to work. The work he determined that he wanted to get into was growing marijuana in the Redlands, to

cut out all the transportation hassles. He wanted to experiment with cross breeding to cultivate hybrid strains that were better than what they had been bringing in from Colombia. He wanted to grow killer weed.

Chapter 20

A Smuggling Vessel That Had
A Bad Prismatic Coefficient.
The Story Of The Golden Eagle.

After searching around, Butch, Otis and Chili found an appropriate boat for a big smuggling scam. The Golden Eagle was a 50-foot Marine Trader that they found in Harbor Town Marina in Dania Beach, Florida. They paid $200,000 for it.

Built in Taiwan, the boat had twin, Perkins turbo, 165 horsepower diesel engines. It had a custom teak interior and was a nice little yacht. It could cruise at about eight to 10 nautical miles per hour, but the biggest and most important feature was that it held 20,000 pounds of marijuana. After expenses, the three new Partners "stood to make a load of money off the Golden Eagle scam," said Butch, "over a million dollars each!"

There is a ratio of how much boat is underwater compared to how much is above the waterline. Butch explained that the Golden Eagle "apparently had the worst prismatic coefficient

in the entire industry at the time, so it rolled [port and starboard] like a bitch and wasn't a very good sea boat."

The boat was bought by Otis, under an assumed name, using the same deal as had been set up for the MJ. Abbey, Butch's crooked lawyer, arranged for the boat to be owned by a corporation out of Guernsey, in the Channel Islands of England. The corporation was owned by the possessor of bearer bonds. "So, all we had was the bonds and the registration and everything was legit and untraceable," said Butch.

The Golden Eagle Starts Its Caper.
The Trip is Aborted Due to a Colombian Blockade.

Captain Dirk had enough excitement after the ordeal with the last trip on the MJ and had retired. Chili knew Captain Jim, from his days working with Jon B. as an off-loader. Jim was a highly-experienced captain who had a reputation as a real cowboy and had made many successful trips. Jim was looking for a big score now that he was dying of cancer.

Captain Jim was infamous because it was said he once crashed a plane that he was piloting in with a load, on the edge of the Everglades. They off-loaded the marijuana and then cut up the plane with chainsaws and brought in a backhoe and buried it where it lay.

The Golden Eagle was crewed by Dirk's nephew who was a great mechanic and Theo, the ex-Coast Guard kid who had been lost at sea and was a well-seasoned and resourceful mate. The boat was provisioned and readied and left for

Nassau in May of 1980 to check in with the Bahamian government for a cruising permit. They made it through bad weather as far as Georgetown, Exuma when they found out about the Colombian blockade. "It really turned us on our ear. The heat was stopping every boat going in and out of Colombia," remembered Butch.

After waiting in Georgetown for a month, they decided to head back to Bimini where they waited a while longer. It was cheaper to bring the boat back to Miami than it was to sit idle in the Bahamas, so that became the plan.

Captain Jim had gotten too sick to continue the trip anyway, so he flew back. The boat needed to be brought back, but no one wanted to be the ones to do the job, because of the potential heat due to the climate of the drug blockade going on.

Jim had been forced to leave his two machine guns on the boat, hidden in the bilge and he wanted them back badly. So, the crew deflated the Zodiac dinghy. They wrapped the guns in canvas and placed them beneath the floorboards. Then re-inflated the Zodiac, stowed it on the foredeck where it nested and chained it down.

Butch also had a pair of night vision goggles that cost about $10,000 back then, and they worked well, even though one of the lenses was broken. These were well hidden, deep in the bilge.

Jim had some friends that were crooked Miami cops and through him they were hired to bring the boat back to Miami, into the luxury island of Key Biscayne, the vacation home of recent president, Richard Nixon.

"On the way, those cops went through the boat from stem to stern," remarked Butch, "they didn't find the guns, but they found the goggles and the bastards stole them. I looked around the electronic repair shops and found one that had gotten them in, to have the lenses fixed."

As he casually knew the proprietor, under an assumed name, from many purchases, Butch learned that it was some Miami cops that had brought in the night vision goggles. "I raised hell with Jim, who got really pissed" and talked to the cops about it, said Butch, "no one was happy, but I got my goggles back."

Butch moved the Golden Eagle over to Miami Marina where it was docked two berths down from a 37-foot Irwin that was used as the home of Sonny Crockett on Miami Vice. "Well, they had this silly alligator that was supposed to be Crockett's pet and they couldn't get it across the dock because its claws kept getting caught in the holes on the dock," remembered Butch. They had to get plywood and place it on the dock, then paint it the color of the dock, to film the scene. "It went on for two days with all the lights and people around and it was interesting, but we were happy when all the people left," said Butch.

Even though he had gotten heavily into cocaine use, Dirk was "forced" out of retirement by doubling his pay to $200,000 and the scam was rescheduled in November.

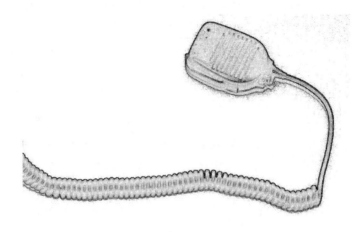

The Golden Eagle Starts Its Caper Again. The Trip Starts Out on its Voyage in November of 1980.

With Dirk as captain, on what would be his last scam, and his regular crew, the Golden Eagle began its trip to Colombia with the standard cruise into Nassau.

The crew dressed better and worked to blend in with the tourist crowds in the yacht areas. "It was a sharp looking boat and it drew a lot more water than the MJ, so it couldn't sneak through the shallowest waters, and needed to work its way through the more heavily trafficked regions," said Butch.

The trip to Santa Marta was uneventful and the loading went according to plan. The trip back across the open water was subject to the regular trade winds and a few decent squalls. "As the Golden Eagle wasn't a very good open water boat, it was miserable in heavy seas, one squall laid it over on its side in the water, all the way up to where the windows were on the cabin," said Butch, 'it was a complete

knockdown with a fully loaded boat and could have been catastrophic, so that was a bit scary."

The yacht went through the regular channels, up the Windward Passage and outside to the eastern side of Long Island and the Exumas. It cut through Staniel Cay, came up across the Bank, went across the Northwest Channel light and just south of Riding Rocks. They skipped Gunn Cay "because it was so narrow that someone could stand on shore and see who was going through the cut," said Butch

While all this should have been normal, Enrique had given Dirk an ounce of coke for the trip and Dirk was doing it the entire way. He was up all 11 days of the trip. "This put the whole caper on unsteady feet," said Butch, "the last thing you need in the world when you're already wound as tight as a god-damned three-dollar watch, is cocaine."

On top of that, it was a full moon the night of the off-load. Everything was going as it typically did for a successful caper. The mother boat was heading to the dark area between Hens' and Chickens' Reef and Davis Reef and the Aqua Sports, with Fish and Ray on one, Wolf and Pat on the second and Tom and Tommy on the third, were on a course to intercept one another.

It was going to take a lot longer to off-load 20,000 pounds than it had all the previous loads that were about half that size. The Aqua Sports would each have to make two trips, with the first one making three and the second standing by in case it needed to make a third trip also.

The marijuana was no longer all down below, stacked up to the windows. "It had been in the three staterooms and the

stairways and the heads, all over," said Butch. "They had already started stacking some on the back deck."

Everything was going to plan. The shoreline was dark, boats had their lights on, out at the reef where they were catching yellowtail. "They were out there just about every night and had been for years," said Butch.

Chili, Otis and Butch were at the Oasis monitoring the scanners and talking to the boats on CB radios. "We were being idiots, there was no reason for us to risk being at the off-load house," said Butch, "but we were planning to leave before the Aqua Sports started coming in.

"It was December 8, 1980, the day that John Lennon was killed. It was a bad night all around," said Butch.

For some reason one of the Aqua Sport captains -- Tom from Georgia -- got spooked by the lights of the yellow-tailing boats. In the tense moments that next passed is when Tom made his statement. He keyed the mic and said what he said, over the CB.

There is No "Plan B."
A Perfect Night for Not Doing a Scam.

Everyone on the Golden Eagle and the Aqua Sports and at the Oasis heard it, with no explanation as to why. "Go to Plan B," Tom said with panic in his voice and Captain Dirk responded that he was going north to Tavernier Creek light. Why he chose to go north and not farther south, nearer the Oasis, is something his coke-addled brain probably didn't even know. But he turned north as everyone on the whole scam looked at one another thinking the same thing. "There was no 'Plan B' ever discussed."

It was before the team could regroup that the Marine Patrol coming out of Tavernier Creek on a routine patrol spied the Golden Eagle and, in the moonlight could see the bales stacked on the stern. Chili, Otis and Butch heard them on the scanner as they talked to the Coast Guard. "We have a bogey coming across the reef and I can see bales stacked up on the stern," they heard the Marine Patrol say. He was afraid to approach the boat without backup. They also heard the Coast Guard say it would be one hour to one-hour-and-15 minutes before they would arrive. "We could have done some kind of diversion, like a mayday call far to the north or south, but the Marine Patrol was on them," remembered Butch.

"Don't worry Dirk, we're going to get you off the fucking boat," said Butch, who then told Dirk and Wolf the plan. Pat got on the radio as Wolf drove.

The plan was impromptu and inspired. Dirk would set the autopilot on the Golden Eagle, then Wolf would pass by the starboard side of the yacht, the far side from the Marine

Patrol boat. Without either boat ever stopping, Dirk, his nephew and Theo would jump onto the Aqua Sport and Wolf would high tail it out of there. That's exactly what they did.

Recovering a Fumble.
Picking Up the Pieces of a Fiasco.

With five big, adult men aboard, Wolf ran up to a little shallow spot near Tavernier Key with the Marine Patrol in hot pursuit. Lights flashing and sirens blaring, it shot at the Aqua Sport to try to stop them. The bullet blew out the fiberglass in the center folding piece of the windshield.

Wolf made a quick 180 degree turn and headed south across the flat. The Marine Patrol's twin engine inboard/outboard drew more water and he ran completely aground. "It was so shallow, he may have torn up the props or even a lower unit," remarked Butch.

"They said in the paper that we shot at the Marine Patrol first, but that was a lie," said Butch, "we didn't even have any guns on the Aqua Sports."

Butch talked to Tom and Fish on the CB radio and told them the Coast Guard was an hour away and there was time to get some of the marijuana off the Golden Eagle. Tom and Fish each went to the boat and off-loaded almost 2500 pounds while the Coast Guard was on the way to the scene. "It was a ballsy, stand-up thing to do," said Butch admiringly.

Chili, Otis and Butch left the Oasis and went to Bo's Keys house, which was nearby.

Wolf also headed to the Oasis so Dirk, his nephew and Theo could get a car and head over to Bo's house. Wolf and Pat stashed their Aqua Sport in a little cove next to the Oasis and then drove over to Bo's place themselves.

The two Aqua Sports grabbed about 55 bales between them with the Coast Guard on the way and the Marine Patrol trying to get off the flat. They headed for the Oasis to off-load then each went back to where they kept that particular Aqua Sport, the crews making their way home.

Bo, who had a plane, arranged to immediately fly the Golden Eagle's crew back to Nassau where they snuck across and just walked out of the airport without checking in (they were still operating on the permits they had received when they first arrived in Nassau). They went back to the same hotel they had stayed in when they had been in Nassau two weeks earlier, in order to establish an alibi. In the morning they reported the boat stolen.

The Coast Guard boarded the Golden Eagle and stopped it, then towed it to their station on Snake Creek and began to off-load it.

"Everybody else just went home..." remarked Butch, trailing off.

The Aftermath.
To Think that They Broke Even
Is a Good Way to Look at It.

At daylight, Wolf broke the rest of the Aqua Sport's window out of its frame, cleaned up the glass and opened the

window so it wasn't noticeable that it was broken. He headed south to bypass the Coast Guard station and then through to the Intercoastal Waterway and went Bayside up to Black Point, where they pulled the boat out and stashed it at someone's house.

The Golden Eagle's crew flew a commercial airline to Miami with receipts of the hotel where they had been, paperwork on the stolen boat and Customs and Immigration forms that showed them just entering the United States. They had an alibi, they were in Nassau.

The Coast Guard traced the Golden Eagle back to the Channel Islands and then to Abbey, Butch's crooked lawyer, but there the trail stopped because of the bearer bonds. Ultimately the new Partners got the boat back and Captain Jim's father bought it and lived on it for about 15 years in Key Biscayne.

Everybody got paid less than they had bargained for and the new partners didn't earn anything. I guess we just about broke even on the deal," said Butch. "That's a good way to look at it," said Don.

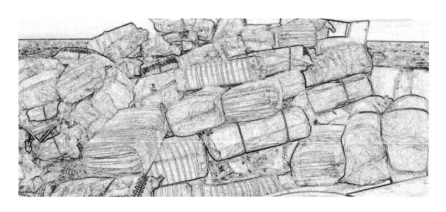

It Was Never a Good Trip
When You Made USA Today.
Preparation Overcomes Panic and Reveals
Stellar Performances.

"When your scam is in USA Today, you know it wasn't a good trip," said Butch, referring to the story, with pictures of the Coast Guard's off-load, that appeared in the national publication days later.

"The guys going out to get weed off the boat with the heat coming -- that was stellar," remembered Butch, "and it made a big difference in paying bills. All the off-loaders and the crew got something, and we had already paid the spic a $40,000 deposit which covered their nut for the load. We had the papers which showed the load had been lost and the old man wrote off the balance. We always paid them first, you never wanted to be owing those guys. It was scary owing them money, they'd come get it," related Butch.

Don didn't get his $100,000 for the rental use of the Oasis, but that hadn't been an incremental cost. The important thing to everyone involved was that none of them got busted. No

one blamed any single individual. They all said that cocaine and bad luck caused the loss. "Not one person went to jail or even got in trouble," said Butch, and that was due to all the time, planning and preparations put into the scam." Maybe there was a "Plan B" after all.

Chapter 21

Trophies from St. Thomas.
The Partners Take A Fishing Vacation.

ISLAMORADA, Florida, with Don – If the DEA catches somebody in the smuggling business they always want to find assets and the defendant will, of course, say they spent all the money they made. A look at the mounted trophies and pictures on their wall or in an album tells a lot. Each picture of a monster fish represents many thousands of dollars that are long gone, but long remembered.

After his last flying trip Don rented a condominium in Tennessee to stay in while he worked for a year on the

Panther Navajo project. In between he didn't do any smuggling, but he did do a lot of fishing.

"I have caught every kind of fish they catch in the Keys: Sailfish – I caught 30 in my lifetime and Tarpon, Bonefish, Permit, Cobia, Grouper and you don't even count all the kinds of Snapper," remembered Don, "but I wanted to catch some really big fish. We all did."

Don said, "Roger and Chili and I went on a fishing vacation to St. Thomas for nine days. We fished the Añejo every day, rotating so each of us fished for three days. The others could go along to observe when it wasn't their turn to fish. We could go along or go shopping with the women, so I went on the boat for seven of the days."

They paid $1100 a day to fish when it was $300 a day for the same kind of boat in the Keys. The fishing was good. The competition for boats wasn't.

"We rented three condos side by side at Red Hook Marina," said Don. "It was the only time I went on a vacation with my partners, because they were still pretty much normal back then. Roger still looked like Charles Manson but at least they weren't so flamboyant and outlandish. Later I wouldn't even go into a 7-11 with them and Chili was my best friend."

Each of the three partners caught two Marlin on the trip. Don's two were both Blue Marlin. He had whole mounts made of them and hung them on the wall of his patio at his home near Homestead. These fish were all in the 350- to 400-pound range. Don wanted to catch a 500-pound fish, so he headed to Kona, Hawaii.

Chapter 22

Marlin Fishing In Kona.
Catching Three Big Fish On A Hawaiian Vacation.

Don arrived in Kona, Hawaii on May 15, 1980. He remembered the day because on the news that evening was the story that the Mariel Boatlift had started. This was when Fidel Castro opened the borders of Cuba and let everyone who wanted to leave, or who he wanted to leave, go. Footage everyday showed thousands escaping the communist dictatorial regime. Don said, "The national news showed a stream of boats being pulled on trailers to Key West for people to disembark, heading to Cuba to pick up friends and relatives."

"We were in Hawaii for two weeks, doing touristy things, going to Luaus, sightseeing and fishing. We took the helicopter tour to view the volcano and they took us over the forest where pirates grew marijuana," remembered Don, "And, of course, we tried some Kona Gold reefer. But, the best part was fishing for six days."

Don caught three fish. He landed a 125-pound Pacific Striped Marlin, a Blue Marlin that weighed 177 pounds and the fish of a lifetime, a 533-pound Blue Marlin. He used Kona lures which are an artificial lure capable of being pulled at high speed – so you cover more ground. It has a concave head that creates a large, distinctive bubble trail that mimics a disabled fish. It looks like easy pickings to a big fish.

"We always released the fish unless we were going to have a trophy mount made of it. But in Hawaii they said that the fish belongs to the captain and they sold the meat for cat food for 25 cents a pound. It was like their tip. Now everybody releases the fish," said Don.

Chapter 23

Fishing St. Thomas On the Pot O' Gold.
Roger Never Let His Money Accumulate,
Some of It Went for Sportfishing Yachts.

Don said, "We had made some money and Roger had bought a used Hatteras for $175,000. He fished it and decided it didn't raise fish good enough, so we made some more money and he bought a brand new Rybovich 58-foot, deep sea fishing luxury yacht for $250,000. That's like the Cadillac of Sport-Fishermen. It had shag carpeting and central air conditioning."

"I told Roger about the Kona lures and in July of 1981 Roger took it to St. Thomas to Red Hook. The Blue Marlin come through there from the full moon of July to the full moon of August. The best time to catch them. They are only there for two months. Roger rented a condo for himself and another one for his crew.

In two months, using the new technique, Roger caught 100 Blue Marlin, a record all over the Bahamas.

Roger caught all his fish using these Kona lures and right after that, up until today everybody uses these Kona lures I first told Roger about. After that he was burned-out on fishing. So, his boat was available. I went down for two weeks and fished 11 days and caught six Marlin.

Onc day I hooked a Marlin and a yellowfin tuna at the same time. I fought the tuna while the mate held the Marlin letting out line to, hopefully, keep him away from the tuna.

The Marlin headed straight out from the boat, jumping, dancing on its tail.

The tuna sounded, heading toward the bottom of the deep blue sea, powerfully pulling the boat along.

"The mate and I were dancing around as much as the Marlin, shouting directions to each other trying not to get the lines crossed," said Don.

"I was exhausted from catching the tuna," remarked Don. "Then I fought the Marlin. We caught and released both fish. So, I caught a tuna and the Marlin during the same episode. The Marlin comes out of the water and you can use the boat to back down on him. The tuna always sounds."

It is rough seas all the time in St. Thomas, something around six- to 10-foot waves and the ride out to the ledge they fish over is an hour. "In Kona, hell, we were fishing like 400 feet off the shore," remarked Don.

"I saw the Añejo I had fished off of before. It was a 43-foot Bertram and it was coming all the way out of the water as it went over the waves," said Don.

"I said, I don't care how many fish they catch, I'm glad I'm not on that boat today. Well they caught six fish that day. Yeah, I would have been on it for that. We caught three which was the biggest day for us," remembered Don.

Roger entered me in the Boy Scouts Marlin Tournament. We used 130-pound test, so I went to an 80-pound test line, so I would get more points for the fish. We could back down on the fish. I caught one fish during the tournament.

Another famous tournament is the Gold Coast Sailfish Tournament that is now called the Presidential Tournament.

Well, a mate wrote a book called "Tournament" that they were trying to get made into a movie.

The Academy Award winning actor, Lee Marvin was interested in doing the movie and he came down to see the situation. "He was with his wife, or girlfriend, I guess and a group of friends. Marvin knew Roger from other tournaments and took the boat on the last day that I could have fished before I left," said Don.

"Marvin had caught Black Marlin in Australia," Don remembered, "He wanted to catch one of the bad boy big fish of St. Thomas, but he wanted 130-pound line instead of the 80-pound I had been using. But, he used the 80-pound."

Don told the story, "Marvin hooked up a fish and while he was fighting it, a shark bit off the body right behind the gills. They brought it in and the head and bill alone weighed 190 pounds. They estimated the fish was 700 pounds. So, just imagine how big the shark was to bite through the Marlin in one chomp. It wasn't like he gnawed him, it was one bite"

"That night we were all in the restaurant. He was at the next table with all his friends and I was with my crew. We were all drinking Bushwhackers and talking back and forth. He said that he would have gotten it in faster if he had used the 130-pound line and it would have escaped the shark."

"The next morning, I came in and he was sitting there, passed out drunk. He got bushwhacked. It looked like he was doing a live version of that movie he was in with his drunk horse. I said that maybe he wasn't acting in Cat Ballou," Don said with a laugh.

Chapter 24

Catching A Monster Tuna in Bimini
With Ernest Apologies.

"Josh K called me one day and said they were catching really big tuna, like they hadn't caught in years" said Don talking about a captain he knew from Islamorada who was fishing in the Bahamas. "I had plenty of money and a flexible schedule. So, I rented a house in North Bimini right next to the famous Compleat Angler pub. I got it for a week for $1000 a day. I headed over to try for a monster tuna. The captain and the boat were another $1000 a day. I had already caught nine Blue Marlin in my life, but a tuna was said to be a real fight. It haunted me... a little."

"Wolf went with me and we each caught a tuna. Mine was 585 pounds," said Don.

They didn't have the fancy plastic gloves like they do now, so you could tell the mates from their hands which were all cut up. Scarred from infections from the fish fin lacerations. They did have Styrofoam coolie cups to keep the beer cans cold.

They fished for tuna on deep-water boats with high gunnels for heavy seas, sloping down at the back fishing-deck with a tall tuna tower undulating skyward for a spotter to see the fish. They trolled for them fast, at about 10 knots, cruising in a big "S" shape.

"The tuna come in from deep water, a couple of thousand feet deep and they swim in about 50 feet of water off Bimini or Cat Island," said Don. They were heading north up to

Gloucester where they caught them, and they were much bigger by the time they got there.

"A whole school of them would be there, swimming in. You could see them from the tower and even from the bridge. It looked like a school of Volkswagens. They were that big! There would be more than one school of them."

The mate in the tower would spot the school and point them out. Although the captain can operate the boat from the tower, you can't really watch the fish and drive at the same time. The mate in the tower was really good at sighting the migrating tuna and determining where they were heading so he could direct the boat in front of them.

"You would put out one pole with a little ribbon on the line that marked how far you put it behind the boat." explained Don. "They drove in that 'S' pattern, trolling fast. Of course, a barracuda would bite the bait fish in half and I had to reel in really fast at that trolling speed on this broomstick-looking rod that had a big reel with 130-pound test line with the drag set really tight. They'd re-bait the hook quickly so I could feed another one to the 'cuda. And I'd hurry to do it again before the fish got there. The tuna won't bite it if the bait isn't whole and doesn't look alive. I did this, three or four times before I hooked up with a tuna."

"I had fought Marlin and I haven't even told you how tough that is," said Don. "You put your legs against the bottom of the foot brace on the pedestal chair, bend your knees sliding down in the chair, then slide up by stretching out your legs as hard as you can as you pull up on the pole then release it down and pull back up and try to take up some line while it is slack for a tenth of a second. This was the

hardest fight I ever had in my life. When the tuna hit I was already exhausted from cranking in the bait and replacing them."

"I had a bucket harness on and a line connecting me to the rod and reel and I wasn't really connected to the fighting chair." Don said, "There was heavy 250-pound line that was attached to 30 feet of steel leader.

When the tuna hit the bait, it pulled me up out of the fighting chair and straight down over to the gunnel, so I was looking down into the water and I felt like the pole was going fucking overboard to the bottom with my ass tied to it." If he'd had time to consider it, Don might have thought that his day among the Islands In The Stream was about to turn into Death In The Afternoon.

After an hour-and-a-half the tuna had pulled the boat back to the deep water. Don said "We were in 2000 feet and he decided to make his death run." Which they call it, because somebody is going to die when it is over, but it still wasn't decided if it was going to be fish or man. "Get 'em up, get 'em up, that means a shark is after him, get 'em up before the shark gets him," repeated the crew, sounding panicked, yelling all at once.

The fish sounded in a powerful, unrelenting spiral downward.

Don screamed, "A shark? This is a fucking five-hundred-pound fish! The size of a small Buick! And a shark is after him? How big is the fucking shark?"

The tuna was running for its life and all the line Don had slaved for an hour-and-a-half to claim, whilst the crew doused him with water to try to revive him, regurgitated back up,

singing out to the depths and the wax on the line was flipping up like pellets of confetti "all over me and my face and my glasses and my eyes.," remembered Don. And the crew is still screaming, except louder, "Get him in before the shark eats him. Get him in!" And Don is chanting a mantra, "Oh, Fuck! Oh Fuck…"

"Now I'm really cranking on him for all I'm worth, which is considerably depreciated since I began," said Don. "I get him up and we used a flying gaff, which is a big gnarly-ass metal meat-hook kind of thing, on the end of a heavy pole, with a big rope tied to it and a cleat on the boat."

"After two hours I had gotten him close to the boat and we gaff him. And that's an almost caught fish," said Don. "Almost. Except we had to get him through the tuna door and onto the fishing deck. So, I was on a block and tackle rig next, trying to get him into the boat. One of us was damn sure ruined."

"We brought the fish into Bimini. The Bahamians were standing there with big sharp knives, sharpening them right there and I'm yelling to them," said Don. "Wait, Wait, we've got to get pictures. Not yet!" said Don. And the captain stepped in. And told the people to wait until they got all the pictures they wanted before they started butchering this huge fish. "We got our pictures and we gave the massive fish to the island," said Don. "So, we fed a good portion of the hungry on Bimini that night. And that was good."

Prologue to Section 5:

When the World Is Ready an Idea Will Succeed.

Don was sure that marijuana would be legalized nationwide in the very near future. He established a state-of-the-art growing operation that developed modern methods, maximized profitable yields and created hybrid strains of killer marijuana. The techniques are now being used today. Don was working in 1980. He was nearly 40 years too soon and the Feds made it their business to remind him that he was way ahead of his time.

Section 5

Chapter 25

The Farm:
The Future of the Marijuana Business Might Be Right at Home.

ISLAMORADA, Florida, with Don, Lefty and Mrs. Lefty – At the time, Don felt the future of the marijuana industry was going to be in growing houses already in the states. "It should produce a higher quality product that was already here, thus reducing half the wholesale cost, that of the transportation," he explained.

The plan was to grow killer weed right in the Redlands and Don started in 1981, with the acquisition of a house on a long, skinny, three-acre parcel that had once been a Mango grove. It was fenced, and a Ficus hedge was planted around it for added privacy. "I paid $80,000 for the house and grove," he said, "and Chili split it with me."

Lefty, who sported a scraggly beard and who wasn't actually left-handed, owned a similar-sized nursery and landscaping business in the Redlands and had done the landscaping on Butch's and then Bo's houses in the area.

"When Butch introduced me to Don, he was being Gomer," said Lefty, "he was talking with a pronounced Tennessee accent about relatives in Nashville. After I worked with him for a while he told me his name was Don and the accent mellowed out."

Lefty was hired just for a part-time project to design the greenhouse without ever being actually told what the crop would be, but he nonetheless developed a purpose-built facility that would produce nearly a quarter-acre farm that would hold thousands of plants.

The greenhouse was about 120 by 100 feet, made up of five Quonset hut hoops and covered by Monsanto brand, green-tinted plastic that had to be specially ordered back then. This let the sunlight in, but authorities in a helicopter couldn't see through the roof. It had drip irrigation with a spaghetti tube emitter, so it put the same amount of water on all sides of the base of the plant.

The sides of the facility used ground-cover cloth which had a tight mesh, so no one could see in. This cut down the air flow, so large greenhouse fans were installed to move the air. A side area was six-feet high, with a mist house to start the cuttings and seedlings. The plants were then transplanted into the ground to grow. The seeds were obtained through mail-order from Amsterdam and sent to someone else's address.

The entire structure was professionally fabricated and installed by Acme Greenhouse, a Homestead firm that is still around today, but isn't and never was called that name. They had booths at trade shows and a big photographic catalog of their installations showing what they could build for you.

Acme didn't know what was going to be grown in the greenhouse, but their catalog had lots of pictures of similar greenhouses and they didn't know what was going to be grown in any of those either. The cost to build the greenhouse was $20,000.

It had a multiple-timer system that watered the plants during the day, plus a second one that was adjustable, so it could mist the plants in timed increments appropriate for the season of the year, the temperature and wind. "It was set up to do it right," said Lefty.

"I had the book, "The Marijuana Grower's Handbook," by Ed Rosenthal that I called the Bible," said Don "and I had been experimenting with some plants on my own. I had Peggy's two sons to support, so I thought I could put them to work in the grow house."

The Hemorrhoid Brothers.
Between Them Were Four Handfuls of Trouble.

Peggy's younger son was big. He was a braggart called Little Hemi, or Roid who could work hard, but not two days in a row and was mostly just in the way, and the older son was bigger. He was a full-time derelict named Big Bobby who lived at the house and was supposed to be the guard. Collectively, they were called the Hemorrhoid Brothers. "Today, they might be diagnosed as somewhere on the learning-disabled spectrum," explained Mrs. Lefty, who had been a teacher. "They fit the mold." Back then they were called pains in the ass. "They were just bad boys," she said.

The Brothers were Quaalude gobblers who like to stay stoned, drink beer by the six-pack, were forever wrecking vehicles and got in trouble all the time. "In between was a study in their misadventures of deviant behavior," said Mrs. Lefty.

Scott, who ran the Oasis and dealt with many personality types, refused to work with them. When Lefty, who politely called them culturally deprived, started handling the grow house Peggy thanked him personally for putting up with her kids.

The $5000 Junkyard Dog.
A Famous Guard Dog Was Everything
He Was Advertised to Be.

The Miami Herald had a proprietary and award-winning Sunday supplement called Tropic Magazine that was known for an eclectic range of story topics. One Sunday its cover featured a photograph of a snarling Doberman Pincher with the title: "The Meanest Junkyard Dog."

Don tracked down the security-animal firm that owned the dog and bought him for $5000, as well as a female mate. The dog was named, not unexpectedly, Killer and he and the bitch eventually had six puppies.

SMUGGLERS' TIMES:
Smuggling In The Days Of Marijuana Prohibition.

"The female was a trained guard dog," explained Don, "Killer was just crazy," and as mean as the article had claimed.

"The idea of the dogs," Don said, "was that only one person would be able to handle them and that would protect the property," Big Bobby was to be that one person. "It took him two months to get where he could bring the dog around." The animals were kept penned up when other people were at the farm.

"I was there for long hours every day," said Lefty, "I kept food with me to distract him, so I could get around. It was not a trustworthy dog."

Chapter 26

The Grow House.

Using Techniques and Procedures Just Being Redeveloped by Today's Legal Growers.

About a year into the growing venture, tropical storm Dennis inundated the Redlands with 20 inches of rain and flooded the greenhouse.

"They asked me to come over," said Lefty, "and I went by just to see their difficulties. It was a sad-looking sight, I felt sorry for the guys."

"We saved what we could. We had big Sativa plants, eight or 10 feet tall that were planted in the ground. We were pulling them out," said Don. They brought them to his home, not a safe house, but the place where he lived, in Homestead. There, he had two shifts of people working at the house, trimming or 'clipping' the buds trying to salvage the crop.

Don said that he had never estimated how labor-intensive it was, having to trim the buds of the excess leaves. "The Colombians did it with cheap South American labor costs," he remarked.

"We saved the trimmed leaves. I sold them for $25 a pound," laughed Don. The first crop had revenue of about $150,000 and total costs of nearly $100,000.

Partly due to sympathy toward their plight, and partly "because I saw the big boys making big dollars," Lefty joined the team as a trained horticulturalist, to run the growing operation while maintaining his own business.

Don and Lefty made a trip to Roger's home where Roger provided them with six, and only six, Indica seeds. From these, Lefty was able to grow seedlings, take cuttings and collect seeds to germinate other plants, cross breeding the Sativa and Indica strains, thus establishing the whole production that filled the greenhouse.

"We were able to get three to four harvests per year out of the plants," explained Lefty. "They produced a big, fluffy, airy bud. A gallon size bag only weighed about a quarter-pound." They put the buds in the bag, "with a particularly large bud we called a 'Donkey Dick' on top." It made a nice presentation of the product.

When these were sold the team always referred to the pot as Gainesville Green, so a buyer thought it came from that area and "were not tempted to follow us to work," to find out where the growing operation was located.

The home and an area of the greenhouse was set up with strings to hold the buds, with a humidifier in there to dry them. "You had to be careful not to get them too crisp and dry them out," said Don. The clippers did the tedious and immensely boring job of delicately clipping excess leaves, turning the bud, clipping some more, and repeating, until each bud was manicured.

"Don was paying clippers $10 an hour and that was more than I was making as a teacher, so I resigned my position and started clipping," said Mrs. Lefty. Don's girlfriend Peggy, Juan who had loaded boats in Santa Marta, Pat who was a mate on an Aqua Sport, a friend named Bassett and several others all did stints as clippers.

"We were doing the same thing in 1981 as they are just now doing in the legalized medicinal and recreational marijuana markets," said Lefty, who would know because he has visited legal facilities in Florida. "We were cross-pollinating the plants and created hybrids using male Sativa plants and female Indica plants. The first generation was F-1, the second F-2, and so on…we were on F-7.

The State Inspector.
The Nastiest Inspector in The Territory Shows Up.

One day, as a clipper was arriving at the farm, a State Inspector, who was supposed to inspect every plant nursery in the area, caught him at the gate and wanted to come in to inspect the facility. The clipper said to "wait a minute, you're going to have to talk to Lefty," who then came out to the gate.

"I knew his reputation," said Lefty, "and I told him he was going to have to talk to the owner who wasn't there at the time." The inspector demanded to know who the owner was. "I told him," remembered Lefty, "'Alfred Bud Clark,' the name of a neighbor of mine, whom I hated."

The inspector said he would be back with the Sheriff and a lawyer and that he would have to be admitted. "I'll tell him," said Lefty.

"It was lucky that the inspector caught someone coming in to work and not going home," explained Mrs. Lefty, "because the smell was so strong. You could smell [the marijuana] through the door." She related that the aroma got in your

clothes and hair, and had a definite, distinctive smell. "You left stinking," she said.

Maybe the Inspector decided something nefarious was going on and, not knowing the size and disposition of the organization, decided he didn't want to be involved to prevent any retribution. In any event, "He never came back," said Lefty, "maybe I just handle people properly."

The Whistler.
A Neighbor Always Announces His Presence.

The neighbor at the farm was a "cool" guy who always used to whistle when he was out in the yard near the hedge and fence line. "We always thought he was simply letting us and the dogs know 'it's only me,' and that he was the one who was around, and you might hear him," said Mrs. Lefty. The Whistler's wife used to jog around the perimeter of their property most days, so you could hear her moving about.

The Lowlifes.
Idiots on Parade Create Problems.

Don referred to thieves of any stature as "Lowlifes," and a crew of this variety thought they had figured out what might be within the farm compound. "This Road Warrior-looking gang started to come around to the front or back gates," said Lefty. "Usually you could yell at them and they would scatter," because they were seeking the element of surprise.

They made attempts in the night or day. "In any event, I told everyone not to ever shoot at them."

"Once they stole a greasy battery off a diesel pump, to be spiteful," Lefty remembered, "and to piss off the neighbor. Another time they really made a statement when they set fire to a car at the front gate." Lefty said that he assumed it was meant to be a diversion or distraction to allow them to get in the back gate. "Why would you bring heat down on a place where you wanted what was inside that place?" was Lefty's rhetorical question. "The fire department had to come out to put out the fucking, burning car," he said.

Friday the 13th.
The Day It All Went Down.

One day, the Whistler's wife was out jogging. It was May 13, 1983 at about 10:00 in the morning, when she saw six young men with rifles at the edge of her property. She asked who they were, and they said they were the police. Whether they were, or whether they were the Lowlifes, soon enough, plenty of police would be in the area.

The young men approached the back gate and Bassett took a shot over their heads. They returned fire, a lot of fire and "everyone at the farm scattered," said Lefty.

Later, Bassett called Lefty at home to say a helicopter was circling overhead and he would be hiding in the bushes nearby, so please come get him. Lefty drove past, Bassett jumped in and they went back to Lefty's house.

Still later, Mrs. Lefty made a drive down the road where the farm was located. The helicopter was still there, and she thought it followed her home.

By the evening news, the story of the bust was on all the local channels' news shows and it even made CNN. "Media attention is never good in the marijuana business," said Don. "I immediately shaved the beard," Lefty remembered.

A few days later, after Don couldn't find Big Bobby to keep him away, the brother went to the farm to retrieve the dogs and he was busted and sent away to prison for six months. Depending upon circumstances, he could have gotten five to ten years.

A short time after that, the authorities tracked down the name of Acme Greenhouses and asked them who ordered the greenhouse built. They said it was Lefty.

In no time at all, the DEA showed up at Lefty's house when he was watching the kids. They wanted to talk. Lefty asked if they could talk softly because the children were there, and he invited them to sit down at the dining table. "They were polite, I was polite," said Lefty, "they asked questions, I lied – well I wasn't under oath. They went away. I went away for four days. They never came back. Maybe I do know how to handle people properly."

Mrs. Lefty Speaks:
A Word from the Female Perspective.

Butch once spoke about the adrenaline rush that hits a smuggler at each step of the operation completed

successfully. "There was certainly the testosterone side of the work," remarked Mrs. Lefty, who chose to be called Mrs. to accentuate the female side of the business and the wife, mother and caregiver of the home and the children, aspects.

"There was the thrill and allure of the Miami Vice life, of the times and the career choice your husband had made," Mrs. Lefty explained "and the measurable financial benefits, but there was also a very definite, constant fear and worry, and conflict, because the actions could have been punished, because they were against the current laws, and of course there was the wondering if the benefits out-weighed that daily dread and fear."

Mrs. Lefty remembered that when Lefty was out working at night, there was always a pang of panic anytime the phone would ring because she was unsure what the message would be that time. "It was not all fun and games," she said, "especially when something went wrong – you tried not to know what was going on, but the scary part was they came back to my home."

Chapter 27

All The Characters On Stage For A Wedding Party.
Now Retired, The Oasis Is A Beautiful Venue
For A Keys' Wedding.

ISLAMORADA, Florida, with Don, Ray, Chelsea and Gayle -- It's a movie cliché to have a wedding scene in a story to describe all the characters, but it became an obligatory cliché because the situation happens often in a person's life. People who would ignore one another in a restaurant or barely acknowledge the other in a convenience store will show up at a wedding, sit down, break bread and party like siblings.

That's what happened when Otis and Joanie asked Don if they could use the Oasis for their nuptial venue in November of 1984. Don had already decided he would never use the Oasis for smuggling again, so there was no harm in inviting a bunch of people over to have a party at the house. "You can say the same thing about that party that people say about the

seventies," said Don, "If you remember much about it, you weren't there."

Of course, the partners were all present: Don, Chili, Roger, Butch, the best man, Otis, the groom plus just about every associate from their business world attended.

Don was understated. He had said he would loan the use of the house, but that he didn't want to be involved in the planning or administration of the wedding. "I didn't want to have to do anything except show up and party," he said.

Chili, who was about 350 pounds at the time and wearing a huge flowered-shirt, and his wife were there – bickering -- and their son Tito was along. Ray said, "He looked like a clone of Chili, just scaled down to three-and-a-half feet tall." His wife and son left after the wedding before the party began.

"I saw Don and Chili in the woods talking and figured they were discussing some business," said Ray. "No, I was pretty much retired then for a few years, we were doing coke and Chili didn't want his kid to see," said Don. "Here I always thought you were violating the RICO act and you were just getting high," laughed Ray.

Roger, looking like Charles Manson with that bushy, crazy hair and eyes and a scraggly mustache that covered his entire mouth -- so he looked grimy -- was there, wearing a freshly laundered and pressed T-shirt and Captain's shorts with lots of pockets and new Topsiders. Roger was hard to understand when he spoke because he always talked like he had a mouth full of marbles. When he was wasted he became even less coherent. "I liked Roger," said Chelsea, "He's the

one that caught that tiny, little sailfish, about 13 inches long and had it mounted."

"He caught it in a tournament," said Don, "It was the smallest one I've ever seen in my life."

Otis and Butch were each wearing authentic Guayabera Cuban shirts from the homeland and light-colored slacks. It was the first time in months that either of them had donned long pants.

The service was conducted by Linda, who was Scott's wife. She was a notary and could perform weddings. "Although she might have been ordained as a minister by Reverend Rick. He used to do that. He ordained me for $35," said Ray.

"Did they have some kind of special self-written vows, like 'I promise never to smuggle again,'" said Don, "But then Chili would have definitely had a comment on that."

Joannie had on a white flowing sundress with a bouquet of carefully trimmed Bougainvillea flowers of various colors. Her two bridesmaids, Michelle and Susan had on similar dresses. "Michelle's was light blue, and Susan also had on a white dress, and she had purple stockings underneath," said Gayle who was Bo's wife at the time. "Which I thought was different," Gayle added. "Now that's a statement," said Ray.

"Otis was as nervous as a long-tailed cat in a room full of rocking chairs," remembered Ray, "He and Butch were both nervous, this was an event you needed long pants for. Otis told me he wasn't nervous about marrying Joannie, but he was nervous about doing it in front of all those people."

"He was probably right to be nervous," said Ray. "Everyone was heckling them, there was a steady banter going on and Chili was leading it."

"Chili heckled everyone," said Don. "Everyone was spouting out comments trying to be funny," said Gayle who had been pregnant at the time and was completely sober. "I was three months pregnant and had a nine-month-old at home with the nanny, that I had to get back to because I was breast-feeding. I saw the wedding and ate and then I left."

"The whole ten years I was with Bo I was pregnant and then everybody went away so I never did get a chance to party, which is probably a good thing," said Gayle.

There were about 150 rented chairs set up in straight rows going to the dock, looking straight out on the ocean, where the fish hanging arch that had displayed so many of Don's catches was decorated with twinkling lights and flowers. They waited to walk down the aisle until the full moon was rising. "That gave plenty of time for the guests to enjoy the beautiful colors of the ocean to the east as the sun got lower in the west and the colors of everything took on that electric quality -- where it looks like they are illuminated from the inside -- that's so beautiful," said Chelsea. It also gave plenty of time for the guests to get completely toasted and fully baked.

The light, warm breeze was dancing among the palm fronds by the time Bo walked Joannie down the aisle amid catcalls from the gallery. "I felt a little bad for the couple," said Ray. "Everybody was kind of wasted and just trying to have a good time, but it *was* their wedding."

"Everyone was already coked-up and drunk and the coke was flowing, and the booze was flowing, and the pot was flowing, and everyone was kind of swept away," said Gayle. "It wasn't a very serious affair," said Ray. "Everybody was standing in ovals all over that huge yard," said Chelsea, "something was being passed around in each circular group."

Maybe it was an omen that the wedding wasn't taken too seriously, because the marriage didn't last very long either. Before too much time had passed, Joannie wound up with Buck for several years.

A topic of conversation was the very recent trip that several of the guests had made with Butch on the Little Runaway from Coconut Grove to Key West. "That was a horrid adventure," remembered Ray. "That boat did everything but sink."

Don agreed, "It was a fucking nightmare, working around those boats was always a nightmare, but that trip was an extra nightmare. We sailed for two days, tore things up and wound up right back where we had started."

Chris the Wrench, who was no stranger to marine adversity having once run out of fuel in the Berry Islands, carrying a load back from Colombia, was at the wedding. He had been the mate for Captain Tim on the MJ and then had captained some trips himself. "He was about five or six years older than me," said Ray, "He always tried to play the big brother role to me and always tortured me with tasks trying to groom me to be part of the Colombia crew."

"We needed good crew on the Colombia trips, everybody was probably always trying to recruit you," said Don. "I don't blame you for not going, it was a tough trip."

"I could take a night off-loading, here; and a day driving a truck, there -- but 11 days or two weeks sitting on the shit…that was too much for my taste," said Ray.

"It was Wrench that had sent me up to do some task on top, on the roof of the boat and I was doing it and I turned around and that radar caught me right in the face as it came around and knocked me down and I almost went overboard. I blamed Wrench because he was responsible for me being up there."

"Wrench was a good guy though," said Ray, "He was a pretty *"studly* dude" who had a bad ass Beamer that was a screamer. He came home from getting his first cash from being a captain and put about 20 grand, into this BMW. It was kind of an ugly, little square car, but he was a mechanic and he put all kinds of money into it. We had a blast out in Vail together. I don't know whatever happened to him. I went up north and a lot of these guys disappeared from my life."

Don said, "Most of these guys I hid from anyway and when they quit, I *really* hid from them."

Ray remembered that Andy was at the wedding. "He was my pot guy in Indiana." In fact, almost the whole crowd of associates involved in the present and most of the past scams were at the wedding, that included distributors and retailers from across the nation. A lot of these people didn't know each other, but they may have known *of* each other and they were all involved in the same capers. They were all company folks, but many had never met each other. This was on purpose, so nobody could steal someone else's connection. Many of them knew of the Oasis but had never been to it or some didn't even know it was in the Keys.

Bird was there, he was a big, crazy mother. A real tall skinny guy who was really tight with Bernie for a long time.

Of course, Bernie was there. He was the brother of Butch's girlfriend, Shirley, and he helped Butch out a lot. Bernie was a handyman, a multi-use guy who was very resourceful. He wound up in later years drinking himself to death.

Shirley was a windsurfer. She tried out to go to the Olympics back when windsurfing was an exhibition sport, but wasn't chosen. She was at a regatta in Key West which is why the crew had planned to sail down on the Little Runaway the two weeks before on the aborted voyage that wound up back about where it started.

Shirley later competed in a windsurfing regatta in Australia. On the way back, she had a stay-over in Hawaii. She sent word that she was never coming back, and she is still living there today.

Bo bought a lot of Don and his partner's pot. He was of slight stature. He was just a little guy who worked out too much and had an attitude of a really big guy. "He was a bulldog," said Ray. "He was so serious," said Don, "always working."

"He was working when I delivered our first child, Joshua," said Gayle. "He was stuck in Chicago on business and I had to have Dougy drive me to the hospital. "When our second, Shawn was three days old, we went on a trip to collect money."

Chelsea, Don's girlfriend was there, and she has her own memories of the afternoon and evening. "I was so new in Don's life at the time. We had met on my daughter's birthday, August 25, 1983 and dated for six or eight months before I

moved in. So, I'd only been living with Don for about six months or so. Because I got Scuba certified in the summer of '84 and that was after the wedding," Chelsea said.

"We didn't have that many people visiting until we had that big party at the wedding. That kind of opened the flood gates for people coming down from everywhere," said Chelsea, "before that day I just thought Don owned a place that sold trash trucks."

"Yeah, that was one of my little covers," said Don. "You could have been in business with Sal," said Ray, "he looked the part."

"One of my favorite guys of all the associates was there, Sal from New Jersey, he was so funny," continued Ray, "If I said to think of a stereotype of a New Jersey guy who distributed pot in Jersey and New York, he is who you would have thought of."

Don said, "Sal would do a lot of coke and get right in your face talking to you, a mile a minute, and he would have the nastiest breath. I'd say, "Sal, can you tell me that from a little farther back.' He's still around," remarked Don, "Dick was there. He still knows him, but Dick hasn't returned my last couple of calls. He may be back in Minnesota. He moves around a couple of times a year. He never got caught but he is still paranoid."

Dick has always spent the summers in Minnesota. "He hated the winters there, even when he was transporting marijuana up there in the dead of winter," said Don.

Gayle remembered that Lefty and his wife were there. "Lefty was everybody's landscaper," said Don. "Lefty was a front for a lot of people," said Ray.

Ray remarked that the Hemorrhoid Brothers were the main characters at the grow house, but they weren't at the wedding."

"No, they were long gone by then," said Don.

That reminded Gayle of Randy who was at the wedding. "Later when everybody was going away, he just dropped out of sight and vanished. No one ever saw or heard from him again."

Scott was Don's cousin, the husband of Linda, who conducted the wedding ceremony. He was the main off-loader at the Oasis and sold a little cocaine to make his and Linda's use self-funding. Some had accused him of stealing a bail too, but Don didn't think he had. Scott died in prison when his intestines ruptured, and they couldn't save him in time.

Pat and Cheryl were in attendance at the wedding. Pat was the mate for Wolf on an Aqua Sport, off-loading. His wife Cheryl didn't know anything about the business. "The only thing I remember about that girl," said Ray, "Is that she had a pet hog."

"Yes" said Don, "It was a big one, a 200-pound hog, in – the – house! When I was there, I slept on the couch, and when it was 6:00 in the morning, this 200-pound hog wanted to go out. I could hear it clumping on the tile floor, I thought I was going to get gored sleeping on the couch. I said, 'When I'm staying here you've got to put me in the office, so I can shut the door.' She had the hog in the house like it was a dog, I told her that I was going to eat it. When the hog finally died they buried it before they told me, because they were afraid I was going to butcher it and eat it."

Rick was another cousin of Don's and he and his wife Susie were there, and Susie was pregnant. "Rick worked with Scott off-loading at the house and he did a couple of loads," said Don, "But he had a real job and just did it a few times. He brought the load into the stash house and later drove it. Years later we grew some pot together."

Everybody was buying into a $10 pool of what day Susie would give birth and Rick had bought a couple days in a row and the day before the first one of those, he took her for a long motorcycle ride over all the railroad tracks in the Redlands, which are plentiful and bumpy. The baby was born a day later, and everybody said Rick had cheated, that he had bounced Susie around on the motorcycle and got her to go into labor. Some have said that the baby, named Summer, loves riding motorcycles to this day.

Wolf was aptly named, with unruly hair and a bushy beard he looked like a person who would be called Wolf. He was the captain on one of the Aqua Sports who rescued the crew of the Golden Eagle when the Marine Patrol was coming after them and got shot at for his troubles. Wolf was a pretty normal guy until he got really wasted and then his appetite turned to fat women. He would go crazy chasing after a really big woman, the heavier the better. Maybe that is why he and Chelsea never liked each other, she was busy getting thinner and better looking as time went by. "I never liked Wolf either," she said.

Reverend Rick was there with his daily allowance of cocaine in his pocket. He had originally bought the MJ and did two loads, then sold it to Butch and Otis. His day job was selling cocaine and, being one of his best customers, he

would lock his stash up in a time lock safe, so he could only open it once a day.

Ray said he would sometimes hang out with Reverend Rick as they sat around and waited for the safe to open so he could get some coke out. "He'd take a gram or two out and then he'd lock it back up for 24 hours. That's how he dealt with his cocaine addiction, it was a brilliant thing to do. He was a cool cat. He had a little Porsche Boxster that he liked to tool around in."

"He got me into rare coins that we all bought and lost tons of money," said Don.

Gayle said "Melissa and Robert were there, you didn't even know him. He was on Bo's side and he and Bo were really good friends. Both Melissa and Robert got into coke so heavy they had to both go to rehab."

"Is Robert the one who imported legitimate shit and owned the Lady Conch asked Ray. "No, you're thinking of two different people; Al from Indiana with the rugs was totally legit," said Gayle "and the owners of the Lady Conch were Melissa and Doug."

"The Lady Conch was a purpose-built smuggling boat," said Don.

"I'm not really sure what Robert did," said Gayle, "He was a seafaring kind of guy, he went off on boats and went around the world and brought stuff from Australia and the Philippines on a different deal than the one that you all know about."

Don said, "We sold Robert some marijuana, Bo took his stuff everywhere: Kentucky, Indiana, Illinois and Michigan that I remember."

"Robert and Melissa were also part of Bo's group financially," explained Gayle. "They all backed-up the money thing, with the big trucks and the boats and the airplanes. They helped do that."

Steve and Christine were there. He took pot to Georgia and sold it. "What a scumbag he was," said Chelsea. "I don't even want to discuss him, it makes my skin crawl."

"Steve's old lady, Christine was one of the reasons I left you," said Chelsea to Don. "I walked in on you and she and you were having sex."

Don entered a dialog he seemed to have gone through many times before. "We were not having sex," he stated.

"No," said Chelsea, "She was just baiting your hook and the out rigger was fully extended."

"We had been in the hot tub," started Don, tiredly. "Yeah, yeah, how does that make any difference?" asked Chelsea laughing.

Chelsea then said that she remembers the first time she met Gayle.

"I was at a party on the beach in Islamorada when there was this art festival going on and she had the best body I've ever seen in my life. I've told her that more than once. I just never saw anything so pretty and I don't even like girls," said Chelsea who would know, she was a licensed masseuse by trade.

"Well, thank you," said Gayle, "you're not so bad yourself."

"Thank you back," said Chelsea, "We're not too bad for a couple of old ladies." They had been close friends in the day along with Julie who was married to Coconut.

"Yeah, Coconut and Julie were there, and I haven't seen them since," said Don, "Coconut owed me $40,000 and I never saw him again after that except when he introduced me to Little Mike who rented out the Oasis for a year."

"Well, good luck collecting that now," said Gayle.

"I saw him about 10 years ago," said Chelsea. "He was a manager at a Burger King in Pompano Beach.

Coconut was a distributor in the mid-west at the time of the wedding. He was taller than Chili but weighed in the 350-pound range, with gusts to 375.

Don asked Gayle, "Isn't Julie the one who threw all his clothes and her clothes out the window of the Pier 66 Hotel in Ft. Lauderdale at your wedding?"

"Yes," said Gayle, "The next morning there was underwear all over the marina when I got up and all the guys had been evicted from the hotel during the early morning hours for creating a disturbance. It turns out Coconut wore thong, G-string type, size 5X underwear. They looked like little hammocks hanging from the palm trees."

Duncan was also there with his girlfriend. "He's the one that got everybody passports and driver's licenses and birth certificates," said Gayle. "He had round glasses and a big old walrus mustache." Don didn't remember what he looked like but said "I bought a lot of stuff from him. That's where I got the birth certificates that the guys used when they got busted in the Bahamas. They got thrown in jail under fake names. It took $100,000 to the attorney and in bribes to get them bail, which they jumped under the assumed names.

Billy Mo was there, he was a chemistry major in college, and he came up with a sunscreen formula that he and his

partner sold and made a bunch of money. Ray said, "Before that Billy Mo showed up in Indiana to sell pot and he knew one person there besides me and that person wanted to kill him, and I said 'No, no, he's not a bad guy' and calmed the guy down,"

Ray had plenty of connections and was able to move the pot. "So, I got his ass out of a lot of trouble for that. I think I helped set him on a path to another line of work, which was good because he would have gotten killed as a pot dealer."

Gayle said, "You have to be a certain type person and he was not of the breed."

In Islamorada everybody was in the business. "Guys could be working at a grocery store, as a mechanic or on a dock one day and then somebody offered them $10,000 to go out and unload for the night," said Ray, "So it was hard to go back to working at a grocery store, everybody was involved in one way or another, or slept with somebody who was."

Fish was there, he was a good example of that, a couple of nights working changed his whole life. "I don't know what happened to him," said Don, "He was not the kind of guy who would be on Facebook."

"No, said Gayle, "He's the kind of guy who might not be alive right now, he was a hard-living kind of dude."

"He was salty as all get out," said Ray, "But a great guy, I spent many an evening with him. He lived on that old boat with that nasty, scary-ass, old Pitbull bitch named Gail Force. I went over there one day, and Fish wasn't home, and she was in the cockpit just barking and barking, going crazy. I checked out what was going on and she had just had pups and

one of them had fallen down and it was in a bad spot in the boat."

Ray continued, "I think one of the scariest things I ever did in my life was to get on that boat without Fish being there and get that puppy out of the bilge and give it back to the mama dog when she was growling and barking at me. She let me do it and I think I was her friend for life after that. Shortly after that Fish got a different, newer boat."

"At that time, smuggling changed the whole face of the Keys," said Gayle. "This is the truth, the movie theater was free for kids whose dads had gone away, and restaurants, clothing places that were privately owned and hair cutting places all gave these huge discounts to the families because everybody's kids were here, and the smugglers were away, and their business supported this whole town. The mug shot book was all the same pictures as the high school yearbook. And a father-daughter dance at the school would have been a bad joke," said Gayle, quite seriously.

"Everybody that lived in the Keys that was from here helped get the stuff in and anybody that lived in the Keys and was from somewhere else had connections back home to sell to," explained Gayle.

At the wedding there were Tom and Eileen from Tavernier, who distributed to Oregon. The MJ's Captain Tim, who was an unlikeable, weirdly different sort of cat, who was really serious and a complete gun nut, and Captain Dirk who did massive amounts of coke until he had his second heart attack. Tom, who ran an Aqua Sport with his son Tommy and made the actual Oasis bar was there.

Kathy, who lived about two miles away and was in her 70s, could party like someone a third her age. She organized the food for the reception, and Chelsea had something to do with the food. "I had over a hundred and fifty potatoes in the oven for baked potatoes, I had something to do with 150 baked potatoes in the oven for a few hours," said Chelsea. Kathy's Tom, who was so called because there were so many Toms around, was also there and so was Glory, who was a big Russian dude who distributed to Southern California.

Gayle said "There was this other guy, Gordon, who flew in for the wedding. He was an actor in California and sold, out there. He was the tall thin guy with the tiny mustache, his date was a little blonde who looked like she was from California. He was from San Francisco. Bo worked through making the connection with him when we went out there on a family vacation."

"There were two guys who came up from South America at the wedding for a little while but didn't stay for the party. They were real creepy. They were at our house the night before the wedding and they were doing coke with Bo and this and that, and the next thing I knew Bo got out a gun and was yelling and he shot out the TV. He was showing them what a bad ass he was. He was getting across the point, don't fuck me over or I'll kill you guys."

Ray, who is Butch's brother and spent time as a youth at Butch's house which was across the street from Bo's house said, "I remember meeting some fucking characters over there at your place."

"I was with my buddy Andy before the wedding ceremony and we were kind of normal chit-chatting with Sal," Ray said,

"and then it was like 'game-on' with the drugs and alcohol and everybody had stocked up. Some of the guys from up north had brought hash with them and there was plenty of coke and pot and booze; I remember bits and pieces of the ceremony."

The wedding wasn't the big thing, the party was the big thing," said Don, "We had Dom Perignon for the toast and it went all to hell from there."

Gayle asked "What about the captain who now owns the marina. He was there with his wife and her eyes were about to bulge out from shock."

"Mark," said Don, "I see him on Facebook. He won the Conch blowing contest in Key West last week."

"He always was good with the locals," joked Ray.

The party was indoors at the Oasis because everyone said it was too hot to be outside. "There was coke all over the Oasis bar and everybody was pacing in front of it," said Gayle, "Bo never came home that night."

"There was a big spread of food, but I don't remember eating anything," remarked Ray.

"I recall Chili walking around with a dinner plate filled with coke," said Chelsea.

"I remember Lefty was playing his guitar and singing. He was good," said Don.

"Lefty was working for Bo, he was basically Bo's helper, off-loading and helping with inventory at the barn in Indiana and he got busted four years later," said Gayle. "Everybody that was involved got busted."

"They asked Scott to come up there and he didn't want to do it," said Don.

"It's lucky for him that he didn't, and lucky for you, it could have led to your side," said Gayle. "It was shortly after the wedding, that was about the time of Bo's last gig because he got caught. They caught the first guys and it just spiraled for years as one person told on another."

Bo got busted for bringing 50,000 pounds into a barn in rural Indiana. They were picking it up in New Orleans, off-loading the containers and putting them on semi-tractor trailer trucks and taking it up to this barn in Indiana. When he got busted, Bo spilled the beans on just about everyone in that address book of his.

"This old couple owned this big barn in a rural area outside of Bloomington, not too far from this commune sort-of-place called 'The Land,' that was owned by all these old hippies," said Gayle. "They had hand-built houses of various geometric shapes and everybody had their own scene. Bernie had a place there that was built like a pyramid."

Ray said, "I went there for the first time when I was about 12, there was weed and naked girls walking around, and it was awesome!"

"Well, Michelle had lived there with her mom," remembered Gayle, "It was all the hippies living there, she had six kids all from different husbands that lived on the property called simply "The Land.""

When this super big bust went down, there was an article about it in Time Magazine.

There was that whole thing with Dickie Lynn going on about that time, he went away to prison and he got life, because he escaped twice. There's a book about him," said Gayle.

"I remember working at Snook's Hotel and Restaurant [that Gayle and her husband owned] after Bo had already gone and Tom Brokaw did a story about all the people in Islamorada that had gone to prison," said Gayle, "He came into the restaurant and nobody told him that the owner was one of the people who had gone away. Around that time is when the cookbook came out that had recipes from the local restaurants in it and it had a recipe from our restaurant and it said in the cookbook that unfortunately the owner went away. Tom Brokaw didn't know, but the cookbook was telling everybody."

"When we sold it [the hotel and bar], we walked away with only $10,000, we had so many taxes and all the bills that had piled up for the food and booze," said Gayle. "Ten grand, out of the hundreds-of-thousands that went into it. The property alone was worth a million dollars back then. But I had kids to raise alone and I needed the money and the time to earn other money."

"My kids turned out all right," said Gayle.

"Yeah, mine did too, I did a pretty decent job parenting," said Ray, "but it could have gone the other way and I'm so glad it didn't."

"When these kids were growing up all this wasn't available to them," said Ray. "I told my older boys the stories when they got old enough and they're saying, 'you did what?' It's a different time than it was then."

Chapter 28

A Horrid Adventure In More Detail.
The Trip With Butch On The Little Runaway
From Coconut Grove To Key West.

One topic of conversation at the wedding was about the trip with Butch on the Little Runaway from Coconut Grove to Key West. "A horrid adventure," remembered Ray. "That boat did everything but sink. It was a bunch of guys in the cockpit all wasted, a video was set up continually playing porn movies – and not good ones, really kind of grody ones. Music was playing loud, all the windows and hatches were wide open to catch some breeze and we were tacking back and forth in really light, almost flat calm winds, sailing down Government Cut, the shipping channel past the freighters and cruise ships."

Butch was in the forward cabin with his suit case open and all his stuff laid out when we cleared the end of the channel and passed the breakwater where there were big waves. An enormous breaker came through the open hatches and Butch and everything he had brought was swamped under a deluge of water, so it was all soaking wet. It blew the dresser drawers open and washed everything onto the floor. Great way to start a trip," said Ray.

Don said he asked them "How are you going to sail this boat all the way to the Philippines and back? We can't even get out of Government Cut safely?"

"I had a turn at the helm," remarked Don, "and I had the engine wide open and pulled the sails in tight and we were making about four knots. I was fishing a lot back then and I knew the currents in the Keys. Everybody was a sailor but me, so when it was time for somebody else to have a turn, they turned off the engine and started sailing again. They were doing two knots, so in the current we were going backward, losing ground."

Certainly, the sailing was quieter and more relaxing, just the sound of music now turned down, incessant moaning from the porn, the water flowing by the hull -- and the water sloshing in the cabin below.

Water had filled up the bilge into the cabin. They looked, and the starter was covered with water. "There must have been 500 gallons of water in the boat," said Don.

"I just started laughing," remembered Don, "I got out my video camera and started recording the events. They planned to sail this boat all over the world and we were going to sink it trying to get to Key West from Coconut Grove.

Butch and some of the guys decided they needed to change the starter while at sea. "I said why don't you try it once, if it cranks we can get to shore and I can get off," said Don. "Then we hit something with the hull and thought there may have been some damage."

"The bilge pumps didn't work," added Ray "and we had to bail by hand."

"When we finally did come back into shore," said Don "they crashed into the dock and definitcly did some damage. It was a fucking nightmare, working around those boats was always a nightmare, but that trip was an extra nightmare."

SIDEBAR 7

Buck Transported Marijuana from Miami to Indiana.
For Two Decades Buck Distributed to
Retailers in the Midwest.

After the marijuana arrived at the stash houses, distributors transported it to their home territory for marketing to retailers. For 20 years Buck was a distributor of marijuana, a jobber, you might call him in the marketing world. He bought pot from Butch and Bo, and Bo's partner, Johnny, who all knew each other from their college days. He didn't know at the time where the pot came from.

It was years before he met Don. "People kept Don hidden so they didn't get cut out of the deals," said Buck, "Smuggling is a dog-eat-dog business and people are very careful about their connections."

"I once knew a guy who wanted one of my connections, I said that if you give me some short money, I'll tell you," said Buck. "He tried it without me, got busted and went to jail. In prison he got all new connections," he finished with a laugh.

Buck picked up pot from one of Don's houses in Homestead and stashed it at a house in Miami Lakes, an upscale neighborhood in the Miami area.

"As it turned out, DEA agents lived right next door," remembered Buck. "Bo got to know them pretty well, he exercised and ran with them."

Like all the stash houses they rented, the place had a two-car garage to facilitate unloading and loading. "We would bring the car into the garage and in a couple of minutes the work was done, and it was ready to go," said Buck.

The DEA agents even invited them to their New Year's Eve party. It was there that Bo lost his address book that had all his contacts in it. He had put the names and phone numbers of all the people on the food chain that worked with him, in the hands of the DEA. Maybe it was foreshadowing.

Joanie, who had married Otis, was now with Buck. "After she divorced Otis, we were together for about five years," explained Buck. She went up to the hosts and asked if they had found her address book. They hadn't yet, so everyone looked around. It was found and handed immediately back to her. Cancel red alert.

In the early 1980s, Buck planned to open a pants store in Lexington Kentucky. Bell Bottoms were all the rage and he could buy them for $2.50 each and sell them for $5. And "people would buy like five pairs at a time." After a fight with his business partner, Buck decided to open his store in the

next closest big college town and that was Bloomington, Indiana, the home of Indiana University.

The location of the store was right across the street from a rehab center and a 24-hour restaurant. "We were always open also," said Buck, "Our motto was 'we never close, but we may doze,' so we became a hang-out."

"We gave a free beer or package of rolling papers to every customer for each pair of pants they bought," said Buck. "The people that chose rolling papers would get to talking with me and I'd turn them on to Butch or Bo, to buy pot. Being an ex-hippy, one day I decided to make some money myself."

Buck would transport about 300 pounds of marijuana in Ford LTDs the forerunner to the Crown Victoria, that had huge trunks, from Miami to Indiana where he would sell it to people who took it to Kentucky and Illinois, among other places. Bo and Gayle would meet him at his cottage on French Lake in Indiana, for a relaxing trip and to collect the money.

I put big air shocks on all the cars I used to transport, so it wasn't obvious they were carrying a load," said Buck, "I also carried a spare air pump just in case the shocks lost air."

"It was a big risk taking it up north," explained Buck. "Anything could go wrong. I lost a truck one time in Florida because the driver messed up and didn't follow the directions to get off to avoid an agricultural inspection station. When he went past it, he got stopped and caught."

"It cost way over a $100,000 to get him off. My lawyer paid a West Palm Beach judge $50,000 to fix it. She was a

big, old fat lady. How she got it done, I'll never know. She said he would be convicted and then have the conviction overturned on appeal. The driver was pretty freaked out when he was convicted. But he won the appeal and the problem went away."

"The judge had a heart attack during that time, but she had set it up, so it didn't impact her plan," said Buck.

Using mostly cars, but a few trucks and even a camping trailer, Buck was happy to work with Don because he had consistently good marijuana."

Once he brought back 1200 pounds of pot that didn't come from Don's crew. He used a 28-foot, pop-up style, high/low camper trailer and stored the product in a big barn he had on his property. "It was bad stuff," said Buck, "I strained it through a tennis racquet. I couldn't sell the shit, it was a bad deal, that just didn't work."

Buck said he told the supplier to take it back. Finally, they rented a bulldozer and came out and buried the load. Usually, he got good stuff and he had a good group of clients.

Some clients from Phoenix would take 500 pounds at a time for three trips, on the arm. Returning in about a week with the money and taking another load. They were two retired bus drivers in their 70s that drove a big Lincoln and made their trips like clockwork.

Sometimes things went terribly wrong and quick thinking and luck were all that avoided a fiasco. A case in point was the night Buck's girlfriend was driving a Ford LTD with 300 pounds of marijuana in the trunk. She was following Buck who was ready to take action to avoid trouble. Near the house

they saw a deer in the road, right by a police car that was off to the side watching the curve.

Buck pulled over and stopped, turning on his interior lights and putting on his flashers. He walked over to the police car and asked what the officer was going to do about the deer that had been in the road and was now nearby representing a danger to traffic. "While the cop was probably wondering what kind of goofball I was, my girlfriend drove by, unimpeded, and went on to the house," said Buck.

Upon arriving at the home, his girlfriend was waiting on the porch. There were warrants attached to the door saying that the house had been searched and to contact the Sheriff's Department. "They found scales and bags, but the only marijuana they found was one joint," explained Buck. I stowed the marijuana at another safe house and told my girlfriend, 'I can get you out of jail easier than you can get me out,' so she went down and turned herself in. It was the last time I was ever at that house. We hired a lawyer and he got her off with a $50 fine, and a big attorney's bill."

Buck's day-business was buying cars at auction wholesale and selling them to buyers at retail, or slightly below. He specialized in Volvo. When the car was over $10,000 which would require a paper trail if the buyer paid in cash, he would accept money orders or cash and fill out the paperwork at a price below $9995. "It was a good business if you remembered to just spend the profit and not the principal; girlfriends sometimes forgot that."

Over the years he sold Don and his crew about 20 cars. Some of the cars were huge-trunk models used for business

and some were for staff members who had just received a cash windfall after a successful caper.

"The Postal money orders were great, they never expired," said Buck, a few years ago I found a stack of them in a coat pocket. It was like $15,000 so it was a pretty good find."

When Buck decided to retire and devote all his energies to the car business, he worked out a deal to give all his connections to a close friend he had known since he was 14. After dinner one night they were walking into his house when DEA agents descended upon them. They arrested the friend and took Buck aside to interview him.

"Is your name Buck?" they kept asking harshly. "Does it say that on my identification?" Buck kept asking back. It, of course, said a different name on the identification, because "every name was an alias," and Buck's name wasn't Buck. After a few minutes, they said Buck could leave. "I got the hell out of there before someone decided I might be called Buck, and that was my last night in the business."

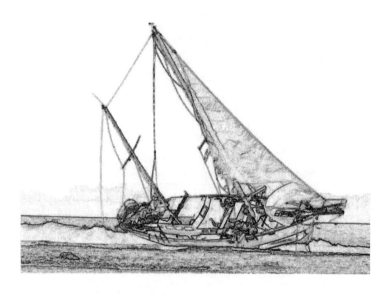

Prologue to Section 6:

Any Venture Will Take Longer Than Planned.

A caper in the Pacific that sounded interesting turned into a two-year odyssey of a life time. A seemingly governmentally-sanctioned scam yielded $9 million worth of merchandise safely in California, ready for distribution. With Stinger missiles delivered to the Afghan rebels, weaponry that immediately changed the tide of their fight to remove a Russian yoke from their necks and started the cracks that led to the fall of the USSR. The movie Charlie Wilson's War recounts the story but doesn't tell how the missiles came to be in the hands of the Mujahedeen.

SMUGGLERS' TIMES:
Smuggling In The Days Of Marijuana Prohibition.

Section 6

Chapter 29

Meeting Goofy Guys in Wrightsville Beach.
The MJ is Traded for an Ocean-Going Sailboat.

NEW SMYRNA BEACH, Florida with Butch – Butch was
on vacation in Wrightsville Beach, North Carolina, on his
own sailboat, just relaxing and thinking what his next scam
might be. It was here, on the North Carolina coast, that he met
Ray M. and Charlie, some goofy guys who had run away on
the sailboat, the Runaway, in an effort to keep the boat out of
Ray M's soon-to-be ex-wife's hands. They were on the lamb,
having absconded with the boat, due to the impending divorce
proceedings.

With aspirations of sailing around the world, Ray M., who
lived in Tortola, had built the Runaway in the Virgin Islands.
They had laid up the hull at the old submarine base on St.
John's and then moved the vessel to Nanny Cay in Tortola to
finish fitting her with a bit of help from some locals. He had
spent a year-and-a-half working on the boat so far and,
running low on funds, was unable to finish her.

The MJ was a purpose-built marijuana boat that was now
jinxed with a bad record, since the bust by the Bahamian
Defense Force. After that experience it had been retired from
service and was sitting fallow, docked at Summerfield's in Ft.
Lauderdale.

SMUGGLERS' TIMES:
Smuggling In The Days Of Marijuana Prohibition

Over beer, the new friends decided that an even swap might be appropriate for all involved, except the soon-to-be ex-wife, who was making demands for her share of the Runaway. They arranged for the guys to see the MJ and in short order Butch acquired a 58-foot unfinished sailboat with the mast down, that needed some work.

The boat was registered by Abbey, Butch's crooked lawyer in the same way he had registered the MJ and the Golden Eagle before it. The home port was Guernsey in the Channel Islands. "So, we got some salutes for flying a Union Jack," said Butch.

"The boat was a Bruce Roberts designed, extra heavy-duty, ocean-going sailboat," said Butch. "She had a 16-foot beam, a 120 horsepower Ford Lehman Diesel with 17,000 pounds of lead ballast. The boat drew seven-feet of water and best of all, could hold 10,000 pounds of contraband cargo. It was a solid cruising vessel, only thing was, she wasn't finished – I mean the electrical system was mostly extension cords strewn across the floor under the carpet in the main salon."

"The goofy guys knew the history of the MJ," explained Butch. "They made some modifications to change the profile of her, made a run in the boat and I heard they got caught their first trip. They must not have changed the profile enough."

Butch and Otis and their girlfriends, motored the boat to Miami where they did some of the work on the boat for a few months. "We worked on the boat in every port," said Butch.

"In Miami, we talked to Jimmy G and Jon B, the guys that had owned the Sweetie Pie and they had a caper out in the Pacific that sounded interesting," remembered Butch.

The caper was to go to the Philippines, pick up hash and bring it back to California. It would be two months at sea with the load and an opportunity to sail to a lot of really cool places. "We had just gotten an unfinished ocean-going sailboat and while our offshore experience was minimal, we agreed to be part of the scam."

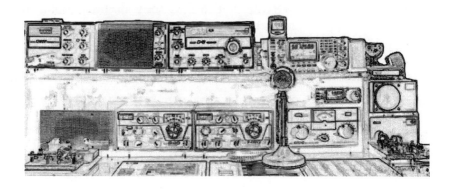

Chapter 30

The Caper Out in the Pacific That Sounded Interesting.
A Year Turns into Two,
Mostly Waiting in Exotic Lands.

The caper was straight-forward. Go to the Philippines. Pick up hash. Bring it back to California. The trip turned out to be delayed, then had to wait for the right weather conditions and took two years in a variety of exotic ports,

Communication, or the lack thereof, had caused problems in the past. On a caper this long Butch wanted to be able to keep in touch with the folks back home. "We decided we weren't going to be without communications on this trip and about 25-grand later, we weren't. We got a transportable Ham radio set-up that could be made operational in about 20 minutes and we were ready to transmit anywhere in the world."

"The set-up was a radio in a Dodge Maxi Van and we put a logo on the side. It was called Publicity Seekers Inc.," said Butch. It had a 30-foot telescoping mast and a directional antenna. The radio had a 100-watt power capability which caused a lot of problems with peoples' TV reception in the neighborhood. It was all illegal and the crew went crazy talking on the radio, back and forth. One time they had a Coast Guard helicopter hovering in the neighborhood where they were transmitting, and it seemed to be looking for the radio transmissions."

Butch said, "A brother-in-law of Jimmy G or somebody met me in a Waffle House in Homestead and gave us the frequency and codes for the radio," so they could communicate with their handlers.

The guy came into the restaurant wearing his motorcycle helmet and a blue tank top. He never took the helmet off during the 30-second meeting, apparently to prevent Butch from knowing what his face looked like. "I was the only customer in the place at the time," remembered Butch, "He just walked in and sat down without saying anything except 'Hi.' I gave him the pass phrase and said, 'nice ink' because he had this tarpon leaping out of the water that went from his shoulder all the way down his arm." He handed Butch the note with everything written down and as he got up to leave, he stated proudly "My own design" he said, and then left. "At least he remained anonymous," said Butch with a hearty laugh.

Chapter 31

The Multi-Thousand Dollar Refit.
The Little Runaway Sails to Newport
For Completion.

"We worked on the refit and had Sailing Services in Miami step the mast and beef up the rig because the mast was a little small, but we never had any issues with it," said Butch. "We rechristened the boat the Little Runaway and decided to sail north, non-stop, to Newport, Rhode Island for the summer." They planned to do a major, multi-thousand-dollar refit on the craft during the warm months and sail out to the Pacific that winter. "It turned out to take until winter and we ended up putting about $100,000 into the boat and another $50,000 in bar tabs into the crew," said Butch.

Paying for bills was always a little dicey. "We tried to pay as we went because we used cash and we kept current so bills never got over $10,000 where paperwork would be involved," said Butch. He remembered early on paying for the final bill in cash at a marina where he had pulled a boat and had worked on it. "It was a sizeable amount and as I handed it over, the owner, who was an old retired navy guy who was Jewish said, 'Oy vey,' taking a deep, resigned breath of disapproval as he watched me count it. He wiped it into the top drawer of his desk."

The sailors for this cruise were Barb, Billy Mon, Otis and Butch and they set out excited about their first big adventure. Butch remembered, "We had hardly done any offshore sailing

at this point, but we had a comfy cruiser that sailed good and we were taking the Gulfstream north all the way. I was really excited, and a little bit apprehensive about the trip – a lot of the systems were jury-rigged, but I figured even if we lost the main engine we could make it. We'd just drift into Newport if we had to. I just wanted to get there!"

The weather was excellent, and they made good time up the coast. About 200 miles off Delaware they encountered a huge Sperm Whale. "It was on a reciprocal course to us," said Butch, "and passed about 20 yards off our starboard. It, was, so, Cool! I think it was the first whale any of us had ever seen offshore and we were psyched!"

"We were still talking about it an hour later, when, suddenly, we saw a school of about 10 giant Bluefin Tuna. They're the size of a traditional Toyota and they crossed our bow. It was an incredible sight to see them plunging through the face of the waves," said Butch.

"Now we felt like we were in a National Geographic documentary. The whole crew was keyed up and on the watch for sea life, we didn't have to wait long," Butch commented.

"Less than two-hours later, we got into a super-pod of Dolphins. For a finale, this was the best show of the day," remembered Butch, "Literally thousands of Dolphins of all sizes surrounded the boat. The noise below decks through the hull was intense."

"The Dolphins were performing for us. We had hundreds stop by the cockpit, leap up, look right at us and do a flip. It was probably the coolest thing any of us onboard had ever seen, to this day."

"Being at sea was always magical for the glimpses and sightings of great wildlife. We all felt it was going to be a great trip," said Butch.

Chapter 32

It's Not All A Nature Special.
The Next Day Reality Sets In.

The next day the batteries overcharged and caused the entire crew to have to sit out on deck for hours until the noxious gases dissipated. Butch said, "It meant we would need to conserve electricity for the rest of that trip."

"Our Loran C, the best navigation system at the time, went out. We were left with more traditional gear: a sextant, an old box Radio Direction Finder and a depth sounder to get the rest of the way to Newport. We did a lot of dead reckoning in those days," remembered Butch.

By now they were on the fourth day of what Butch had figured was a five- or six-day trip depending upon how much of a lift they had been getting from the Gulfstream. "We had been getting a noon sighting with the sextant, so we had a pretty good idea of our latitude," said Butch, "But we were guesstimating our longitude."

Butch remarked that they had the RDF, but those are not very accurate and "the depth finder was a big help because as we neared the coast, the continental shelf was shoaling, and we could see that we were losing depth all the time. About then, as we were bearing down on Block Island, is when we hit the fog bank."

Block Island was their hard-to-see landfall. Interestingly enough, that particular landfall was and is familiar to everyone in the United States who has a Coast Guard Captain's License because it is the demonstration and on the

final test for the navigational skills of the licensing examination that everyone takes. Landfall was somewhat vision-impaired but uneventful. The fog thickened, and they were held up in port for a few days. Distractions in New York further delayed things. Perhaps it was a taste of things to come.

Chapter 33

The Caper in The Pacific Turns into Two Years.
Meeting Interesting People in Exotic Lands,
An Overview.

We knew nothing about Newport, except that it was the home of the America's Cup contenders," said Butch, "Just by luck I picked a boatyard called Newport Offshore for us to base our refit. It turned out to be a stroke of luck for a green crew. It was the very epicenter of the America's Cup action and we ended up right in the middle of it, literally. We were docked between the two America's Cup teams. On our portside we had Tom Blackhaller and Gary Jobson and the Courageous syndicate and on the starboard side was Dennis Conner and his Freedom syndicate. "It was awesome," said Butch, "It was like being in sailboat heaven. Of course, it was so competitive and contentious we could have been mediators, given our location."

"Throughout the trip, we were always changing things around on the boat, so it looked different in different places – had a different profile -- we even changed the color and the crew members, so it wasn't always the same people on the boat over the two years. There are people out there looking for suspicious activity and they can keep track of you. So, you are always conscious that you are on a caper. When we left, we went through Long Island Sound, to Norfolk then to Tortola in the British Virgin Islands."

They left the end of October, after the snows had started and described it as a miserable experience to be waking up on a sailboat covered with snow.

From Tortola it was off to Panama, through the Canal to Balboa. "Panama was wild," said Butch, "because it was Panama." They made a stop in the Galapagos, where they did some touristy things for a few days but also worked on the freezer, then to the Marquesas, to the Cook Islands, to Tonga and then Fiji where they spent a couple of months repairing the transmission and awaiting a new dinghy to be shipped in. "It was a working vacation, they were beautiful locales but there was a lot of torture involved," said Butch. "We made a lot of local friends -- the people of Fiji are fantastic. There was an Asian Pacific Economic Conference going on in Fiji, so there were lots of secret service agents from other countries."

They headed to the Solomon Islands, where there are many war relics and great diving, all the way looking for clouds. "There was no water-maker on the boat, so we had to chase clouds to get underneath the rain to catch water. We would let the first of the rain rinse the salt off the deck, then open the through-hull fittings and catch the reserve tanks full of water in 20 or 30 minutes," explained Butch.

Next, they headed to their first rendezvous point, Rabaul in Papua New Guinea – which was closed. "Volcanic activity, if you can believe it," said Butch, so they were eventually sent to Madang on the Sepik River,

After waiting months in Madang, they were sent to Cebu in the Central Philippines, where they spend five to six more months before retrieving the load. Then it was the crew of

SMUGGLERS' TIMES:
Smuggling In The Days Of Marijuana Prohibition.

Mark, Lynn, Gordy and Woody for 64 days past Hawaii, laden with hash, to California. "That's a really long time for four people to be at sea," said Butch.

Chapter 34

The Original Coconut Chat Room.
The Pacific Net Is The Amateur Radio
Communication Link For Those In The
South Pacific.

The crew of the Little Runaway and perhaps a dozen or so other people across the southern Pacific kept in contact at a specific time each morning measured by Greenwich Mean Time using Ham Radio. Only a few of them talked at a time, but you never knew who was listening.

Mostly they discussed the weather, current conditions at various locations and what the weather might do. News and messages and glimpses from back home, where-ever that might be, were sometimes passed along. Publicity Seeking, Inc. talked with the Little Runaway. Sometimes the messages on the Pacific net were faint requests for something like parts required for a specific engine repair. Sometimes these were loud and clear and other times they were code for rendezvous times and places. Sometimes for multi-million-dollar smuggling schedules.

From the fact that they were talking to Max, the same as the crew of the Little Runaway did, and the context of the conversations, over time it became apparent who else was out there on the job. Rainbow Connection and Seventeen-Point-Six-Five were two yachts connected to the caper. During the tenure of the deal they each suffered career-ending injuries that took them out of the game.

Rainbow Connection came around the backside heading to the Pacific through the Suez canal and got side-swiped by a tanker that cut a hole length-ways through the port side of the hull, ending their trip.

Seventeen-Point-Six-Five owned by a wealthy advertising executive on hiatus was chasing thunderstorms when lightening hit the mast. As the crew affected repairs and one was eyeing the top of it with binoculars, the improbable happened and lighting struck twice, with another charge hitting a second time. It knocked them down, blinding the crew temporarily, and the guy who was looking through the binoculars for days. One of the crewmen who was knocked down received a compound fracture of his leg – weeks away from a doctor.

They were on the radio everyday getting medical advice from doctors and emergency response staff.

The Little Runaway met with its own disaster when it ran hard aground on an uncharted reef one night under full sail. The crew scrambled to lower the sails as the boat slammed to a stop, and they were stuck with no one around to help for a thousand miles in any direction.

At first light the tide was even lower, but they could assess the situation and see just how fucked they were. They rowed the dinghy out to find a path back to deeper water then placed the anchor out and set it. When high tide came they flew the sail in that direction to heal the boat over, so the keel drew less water and they winched the Little Runaway toward the anchor to pull the boat out. After laboriously moving it inch by inch, the anchor was reset, and the whole process repeated with the next high tide. Then repeated again, and

again, and again…for five days before they worked themselves free. In the retellings the days grew longer.

Fortunately, the hull was steel and had not been breached.

Chapter 35

Fiji Is the Crossroads of The Pacific.
It Is the Perfect Place For Recreation
and Equipment Repairs.

The crew of the Little Runaway hit some 50-foot waves heading to Fiji. It was a harrowing experience and tore up a lot of equipment that needed to be replaced or repaired. They did the work in Fiji over the course of a couple of months.

"The people were fantastic, and we did a bunch of work on the boat, like the self-steering mechanism and the transmission, which we had shipped in" said Butch, "We had

a new dinghy also shipped over and my brother, Ray, flew in with equipment we couldn't get and another $50,000 in cash which we needed by now. He even carried a sixteen-foot antenna as checked baggage. We put him up for a while as payment for his time helping us out. He wasn't part of the scam at that time, I'd say he pretty much had the time of his life."

"Fiji is the crossroads of the Pacific," explained Butch, "They service the fishing fleets and the sailors out there, using equipment from the turn of the 20th century. They use this old, primitive technology and turn out the most incredible work. Like sandcasting for metal work. We had a flange made for the transmission and it looked beautiful."

"There was this economic conference going on and there were all kinds of secret service agents from other countries there. It was exciting. We were one of only three boats there, so they gave us a good hard look," said Butch.

"We met some incredible chicks out there and I had a girlfriend while I was there named Shashi that I met in a disco. She was a cute little thing and I gave her $50 as a gift the first night we met. She soon fell madly in love with me. One day she showed up at the boat all decked out in a beautiful formal native gown and lugging about 10 or 12 different traditional dishes she had prepared. She had come courting."

Butch said, "One of the things the girls do is to mark their men with hickeys, so I woke up in the morning and had hickeys all over my neck. I went up to the front desk of the hotel and the woman said you put toothpaste on it -- which is bullshit. So, I'm walking around with toothpaste on all my

hickeys, wearing, like, a scarf around my neck and I know everyone's thinking there's the silly white guy with the toothpaste all over him."

Besides the women in Fiji, there's drink, a native concoction called Kava that is like a mildly narcotic beer made from a root that is pounded into a paste and fermented. "It's a kind of social thing for a bunch of guys – I only saw the men do it -- they sit around with a half coconut shell passing it around until you got bombed," remembered Butch. "It makes your mouth numb, but you really got high off of it. Everywhere you go, they offered you some, the Fijians did it all the time."

Chapter 36

Eyes Are Everywhere.
You're Not Just Out There Sailing with
Your Girlfriend, People Are Always on The
Lookout for Suspicious Activity.

"Loose lips can get you in deep shit," remarked Butch, "a wrong word to someone can get you busted much later... the Pacific is just so big and there are so few places to be, the next spot downwind is pretty much where you are going." He explained that his cover story in the Philippines had been that they were buying custom-made Rattan furniture for hotels in Miami.

"One morning these guys drive up in a military looking Jeep and the guy who turns out to be American came up to me at the hotel bar where I was hanging out reading an old English newspaper. He had two huge Filipino guys with him. Filipinos are usually small, but these guys were really giants, they held back a short distance and the guy began to talk to me. He seemed like he was a bit drunk already."

"He starts telling me that all the generals are on his payroll and their families have safe houses in the states and that he has business going on out there. I told him not to tell me things about his personal business. I don't want to hear this fucking shit," Butch remembered saying, but the guy continued, more-or-less trapping Butch into listening to the soliloquy. The whole "conversation" took nearly two hours.

Suddenly the guy gets up in Butch's face, he didn't have liquor on his breath. "I don't think you are a furniture buyer at all, I think you are full of shit, I think you are up to no good, and we've got a good thing going here for, like 20 years, and we don't want anybody fucking it up," the guy said harshly. "A few years ago, some, ah, *furniture buyers* came through here setting up a smuggling deal. They were flying heroin through here, stopping to refuel on the way to Guam and bringing heat down on our enterprise. So, we shot down the fuckers' plane, and we just aren't going to put up with that shit," said the suddenly stone-cold sober guy who was as serious as a heart attack."

"This whole thing seemed to take forever, by the time he was finished and left, I was rattled. I got the hell out of there, I checked out of the hotel and went to another one," said Butch. "I started hanging out at a different bar!"

"As the scam had been delayed for a whole season, there was plenty of hanging around going on. There were a lot of tall Americans with money there," remembered Butch, "we were trying to be low-key, but it was impossible. At the market you could pick out members of the crews because they were a head taller than everyone else. Everybody knows everybody's business, or at least their cover story. Just changing money into pesos attracted attention. Everybody knew what you were doing."

Butch said, "There was this warlord guy named Morano who ran everything and was said to control about $2,000,000 a month in the laundering and exchange of cash into local currency. The story was that he took a Cigarette boat to Hong Kong every week to bank the money."

"You went to the side of this street stall and you gave them a code phrase, then you went to the back door and into a kitchen with beads hanging from the door, so you could see the three or four heavies in the back room. There was a table full of money and you made the exchange."

Butch said the first time he went, he took a cab and went alone. He needed to exchange $10,000 and wound up leaving with a grocery sack full of pesos. Butch always went with someone else after that and converted less money. "The cab driver was nervous as hell. It was dangerous," said Butch, "because you had cash going in and cash going out and somebody could be clocking your action."

"You never knew who was watching." Butch said that he knew of a couple of guys that bought a boat in Australia and the broker turned them in. They wound up getting busted almost a year later about 60 miles off the coast of California. "They had tracked them from the time they purchased the boat, through the entire scam for all that time and distance, because the broker was suspicious. They thought everything was hunky dory until the Coast Guard pulled up next to them. So, you are always under stress that you were being watched."

Chapter 37

Delayed A Season, The Caper Finally Begins.
A 400-Foot Freighter, Multinational Crew, Freedom
Fighter Objectives and CIA Protection.

Butch had been given the Ham radio frequencies in order to get messages from the handlers about where to meet and when. So, he could also listen to them talk to the other boats and even the mothership. "They were being sneaky, but they weren't being smart," said Butch, "Or they just didn't care."

The Cypress-registered, 400-foot freighter left out of Mumbai, still called Bombay back then, with manageable difficulties getting the crew assembled, disembarking and getting out of town. They headed to Doha where they loaded Petro-coke which is a legitimate, legal by-product of petroleum. It looks like 50-pound bags of concrete and was the cover.

Then, they headed to Karachi, Pakistan where they loaded 80,000 pounds of hash while two black helicopters hovered overhead. "If they weren't CIA, they were somebody with resources," said Butch. The freighter headed through the Straits of Malacca and down toward Indonesia. Jimmy G, who got them the deal, was a crew member on the boat and told Butch stories of the adventures and misadventures many times after the trip was over. He said one of the crew members went crazy and had to be handcuffed to the railing to keep him still, while the event was underway. He got his shit together later and continued the trip. He never said anything to any authorities after it was over.

Down the eastern side of the Philippines they cruised to a spot off Palau. "It was just a latitude and longitude out in the ocean where the off-load took place," said Butch, "A spot of water where $72 million of dollars-worth of merchandise changed hands, and some of that was mine."

There were six boats that made it to the off-load which went professionally. Then the mothership went to South Korea to drop off the petrochemicals and most of the guys got off the boat there.

The story going around was that the whole deal was a CIA black operation exchanging Stinger missiles for Afghan hash through several hands, so the deal wasn't traceable to the Americans. The Russians were winning the war with the Afghan rebels extravagantly, firing with impunity on defenseless villages until the freedom fighters were supplied with the new weaponry that allowed the Mujahedeen to prevail in the conflict.

Chapter 38

At Sea For 64 Days.
Loaded to The Scuppers with Hash.

It was the kind of Pacific crossing where one would wonder how the ocean ever got its name as something that might be calm. The kind of crossing where the crew would have preferred to be anywhere else but there. "The weather was so bad at one point," said Butch, "they had to 'heave to' for a week, so they were in crisis mode the entire time and got blown back 200 miles."

On day 64 of the long, nasty sail, in the summer of 1985, the Little Runaway was off Año Nuevo State Park south of San Francisco. They anchored offshore and waited among some fishing boats for nightfall, so it wasn't so obvious they were just sitting there.

When the time was right, they headed toward some rocks just offshore to meet other fishing boats and big Zodiacs that were used to off-load to the little Park trucks on land. "They had the Parks Department logo on the doors. This was definitely a name brand caper," said Butch. The little trucks took the product into the Park, which was closed and secured, to load the hash into big trucks

"If the CIA was in it on one end, the Park Rangers in uniform were in it on the other end," explained Butch. "There were some Rangers on the team."

A complication and a little confusion for a bit caused the off-loading crew to throw about 500 pounds overboard before

we could calm them down, so they didn't throw anymore away," said Butch.

The hash was in compact bricks and worth, then, $900 per pound. Butch said, "We took it to two houses in Lake Tahoe and sold half in short order. Then it was transported in small batches in trunk loads to Illinois and Miami and even into Canada to sell it. There was no heat on the deal, the CIA was definitely involved, and they screwed us on the payment and only gave us 1000 pounds, a pittance of what they had promised. But who are you going to complain to?"

Prologue to Section 7:

You Don't Lose Your Girl. You Lose Your Turn.

A song says that a woman may get run away but she will come back someday. Don always believed that if it "flies, floats or fucks, rent it!" So, he never wed but had several long-term relationships. "I never got married," he said, "But I got divorced a few times and it cost me the same." His philosophy was not to put himself in the position of having to give away half of what he had, in the present and in the future. "Let me tell you about the women I was dating," said Don.

SMUGGLERS' TIMES:
Smuggling In The Days Of Marijuana Prohibition

Section 7

Don's Girlfriends:
The Women in Don's Life During
This Time Period.

Chapter 39

Linda, Who Wrecked The 'Vette.
Don's First Long-Term, Live-In Girlfriend.

ISLAMORADA, Florida, with Don and Chelsea -- Except as props and boat dressing, women don't figure into the business side of these stories.

"We always kept the women out of the business," said Don. Still, Don had four long-term relationships during the period covered by these stories.

Linda was the girlfriend he had when he first, kind of, invented his job as a pilot going to get the marijuana.

She had shoulder length dark hair, was about five-feet tall and 120 pounds, much of which were breasts. She worked at a bank and met Don through friends of friends and they hit it off. Linda loved to party and that is what first attracted them to one another, but her appetite never quenched and that lead to the break-up.

Don had decided that Colombia was the place to buy marijuana wholesale. He had no connections and didn't know

anybody in Colombia but went on a fact-finding mission to learn the terrain of the Santa Marta area.

He and Linda visited there like any couple on vacation. They flew into Cartagena and drove to Santa Marta, "only getting lost four or five times," remembered Don.

The couple stayed a few days in the best hotel in Santa Marta, a sleepy little colonial beach town with the beginnings of some touristy nightlife.

Not too long after that Linda had moved in with Don, because she was always getting sick with colds and such from the public coming into the bank, Don had her quit the job. "So, before I knew it, I wound up with a live-in girlfriend that I was supporting. I bought her expensive jewelry and then a Corvette," said Don.

She knew what Don was doing with the flights to Colombia, "but she was never involved and didn't help or anything, like some of the others."

A downside to having Linda as a live-in girlfriend was that she liked Quaaludes too much and stole them from Don. Another was that while her inclination toward sex was great, it was not limited to Don. She was having an affair with a girlfriend and was wasted while driving home.

She wrecked the 'vette by running it up a guy wire on a telephone pole. She got arrested for DUI long before it was popular. "This was back when you had to really do some damage to get a DUI," said Don, "like being wasted and running a 'vette up a guy wire on a telephone pole."

Don didn't like that kind of grief or scenes. His mother handled the divorce for him, meeting Linda and giving her money, and telling her to move out before Don returned.

These two lines became part of Linda's history. The fact that she "wrecked the 'vette" being a short hand for the whole scene of taking advantage of a good situation, looking a gift horse in the mouth, so to speak, and "calling Don's mom to handle the divorce" for getting someone else to make a problem go away.

Over time, when Linda needed money, Don bought the jewelry back for what he paid for it, so he paid for it twice, "but at least I had something to show for my money," said Don.

Linda had to go through DUI school and a drug treatment program, but she was gone from the picture.

Peggy Was 20-Years Older Than Don:
A Selling Partner Becomes A Live-In Girlfriend
with Two Problem Kids.

Don was buying Colombian pot for between $300 and $350 per pound in Miami in 1974, compared to $200 to $250 per pound wholesale in Colombia. That hundred dollars per pound multiplied by 1000 pounds was the reason he devised a method to fly down and get it.

Peggy had been Don's partner in the retail by-the-ounce business. She and Bob Z. had been divorced for a while in 1979 when she and Don got together and before he knew it Don had another live-in girlfriend. This one older than him, and with two grown or should have been grown sons.

Peggy had a similar body type to Linda with dirty blonde hair that came from a box. She looked younger than her age, but not enough. She was with Don during the grow house period and worked trimming buds.

Don felt the grow house was a perfect place to put her two delinquent young men to work, but they continued getting too wasted and wrecking cars and needing a lot of supervision. Some think their loose lips led to the lowlifes finding out about the grow house, but Don didn't think it was due to their screw-ups. "They were about useless, but they were honest with me," said Don who rarely has much of an unkind word to say about anyone.

After the green house Don told Peggy he couldn't take care of the boys anymore, and she didn't like the Keys. "We'd had enough of each other," said Don.

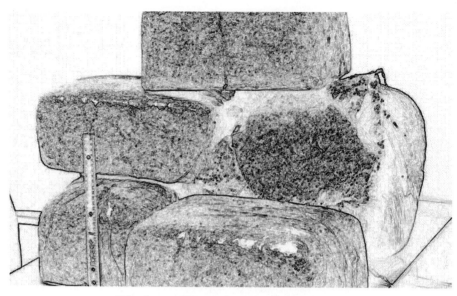

Chelsea Was Going Places.
One Stop On Her Journey Through Life
Left Lasting Memories.

Taller and not as flashy – at first -- as the previous two long-term girlfriends, Chelsea had a good head for figures or a good figure for head, one or both. A tad overweight and lacking self-confidence, she was definitely planning to go places. She was poised for improvement.

A newly minted masseuse, she became extremely body conscious. During the four years she and Don were together, she developed more self-esteem and worked on her physique, getting more fit each year and better looking. Chelsea became more health conscious, gave up drinking anything but water and "worked on liking herself more."

She had two very little girls and before he knew it, retired Don was a family man living in Homestead with vacations

scheduled by the School Board. He devoted his energies to homework and science projects that invariably involved growing things. "My girls are both great gardeners today and know a lot about hybrid roses," laughed Chelsea.

Don was listening to the scanner one day when he heard that the Coast Guard was chasing a plane. Upon looking up he could see it, out over the ocean heading toward the trailer court next door. He and Chelsea, Kathy and Kathy's Tom and the kids all scurried out to the boat and headed toward the plane. By this time, it was dropping bales before crash landing in the shallows near the shore. They could see someone get out of the plane and start swimming away, toward the nearby shore.

When the coast guard boat came closer, the swimmer did a 180 degree turn and headed toward the plane. It said in the paper later that he told the police he was on the shore and had swam out toward the plane to help. It also said the Coast Guard had witnessed the plane throw out 19 bales, but that one was still missing.

A coast guard boat shooed Don and his crew on the Aqua Sport away using its loud speaker – but they were just looking – so the officer left them alone. They were, after all, just another curious family out rubbernecking on an average day in the Keys back then. And they *were* just looking. Don would never let the girls suspect that he didn't sell heavy equipment for a living.

Don had been out walking around the property with his morning coffee, before reading the paper. There in the boat basin, beached on the shore by the low tide, was a bale. He didn't even have to get wet to pick it up. He stowed it in the

garage in an old toy box. It was worth nearly $10,000. Don smiled as he read the newspaper article. He knew where the nineteenth bale wound up.

Chelsea got up to make a big breakfast. Despite putting fresh shrimp in cold water and sitting them on the stove the first time she tried to make them, "They weren't fit to eat," said Chelsea. She became a great cook as well as a frequent gourmet-diner at the area's top restaurants.

"Don would go out and spear some hog snapper for dinner and it took us 20 minutes, like going to the store," said Chelsea. "One time he shot about a twenty-pound hog snapper and gave the fish to me. I held it through the gills, then he shot another one and gave it to me for my other hand. So, I had twenty pounds of snapper in each hand – and I still have those hands!"

Chelsea said the fish couldn't have been any fresher. I remember dipping filets of fish in flour and the meat was still pulsing from it having been swimming a few minutes before.

Chelsea eventually became disenchanted with the relationship and wanted more out of life. She got it one night about three years in to the affair when she and Don were coming into the Oasis early in the evening at the end of a day of boating on the now also retired Aqua Sport. Hard aground on the rocks by the channel of the Oasis was a 32-foot boat, with no one around.

After docking the Aqua Sport, Don waded out to the beached boat. He barely got into water above his knees and could see that the boat was filled up to the windows with marijuana. It was proverbially on his front porch steps.

They sent the girls to an impromptu slumber party at a friend's house. Don contacted a friend named Kathy's Tom and all that long night the three of them took the retired carts and unloaded the boat of its nearly 1000-pound load.

"Don climbed on the boat and I started out in the assembly line carrying bundles from the boat across the muddy shallows and up the rocks onto the shore where Kathy's Tom loaded them onto a cart and pushed them into the garage," said Chelsea. This proved to be too much for her to handle, so she and Don switched places.

They stumbled and crawled over the rocks with the 40-pound bales, "I thought I was in pretty good shape, but I'd swear the bales were 80 pounds and by the end 120 pounds," said Chelsea. They carried them one at a time, trip after trip, through the mud, and both of them wound up all cut and bleeding trying to remember that each bale was worth $8,000 to $10,000.

"We didn't know whose marijuana it was and if they were coming back that night," said Don. "We were scared to death some Colombians with guns would come back and catch us stealing their load. We didn't have any guns or nothing."

The three of them loaded the marijuana into Chelsea's custom van – only up to the windows – but it was still pretty visible. "The van was not made for doing what we were doing," said Don. They drove, twice, with Don as the follow car up to the Redlands, to Bo's house where they sold it to him for the special, "Tonight only price" of $200,000. They had to make two trips without Chelsea ever giving a single thought to the fact that she might get caught.

"When you're that dumb you aren't nervous at all. It never entered my mind that I would get stopped. If I'd been halfway smart, I wouldn't have done it, but there's lots of things, if I've been halfway smart, I wouldn't have done," said Chelsea. "There is a joy to being ignorant," she added.

The Coast Guard towed away the residue-covered boat the next morning and Don and Chelsea and the kids stayed away from the house for a few weeks to let things cool off.

Don summed it up, "It paid off for all of us."

The escapade gave Chelsea and Kathy's Tom each $50,000 and Don $100,000 for knowing how to turn the windfall into cash. Kathy's Tom used his to open a business and Don told Chelsea to put her money in a safety deposit box in case they ever wanted to break up she had money to start over. Don's money went into living expenses.

About a year later, Don was broke, and went back to work in the business, and it was time for the relationship to end. The girls were getting older and starting to understand things. There had been the odd earring left in the shower at the Oasis, some infidelity, a need for Chelsea to be more in control of her life, and a change in Don's fortunes. And of course, "I couldn't get Don to wipe down the shower at our house when he finished showering, but when we visited with his mom he never forgot to wipe it down every time," Chelsea said.

Chelsea bought a townhouse in Naranja Lakes near Homestead with her safe-deposit box money and moved there. She and Don continued to date for about a year, overlapping with the next live-in girlfriend until that got too complicated.

Wild And Crazy Jan.
Only Seeing Her When She Was Partying, Was To Only See A Special Side Of Her.

Don always says that Jan wasn't as wild and crazy as everyone thought. In actuality, she was a pretty normal person, until she did coke and when people saw her wild side, she had been doing coke. There were a few famous stories of her in rare form.

She came as the sun bunny date of a guy visiting the Oasis. She called back the next day to say she left her sunglasses and could she come get them. Soon thereafter she and Don were a couple.

Jan moved in and they lived together for years. She was with him through some of the very good times and some of the worst of times. When the really bad times came, Don sent her home to Kansas, but she kept "unclicking her heals" and coming back and she plays a big role in the second book.

Unlike Peggy and Chelsea, Jan never had anything to do with the business.

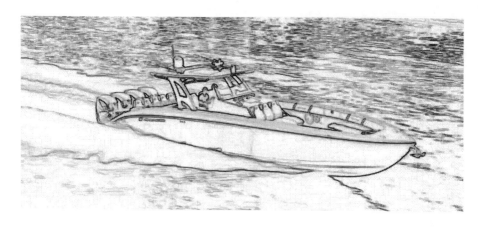

Section 8

Chapter 40

The Oasis Is Rented Out For A Year To Little Mike.
Don's Weekend Living Arrangements
Are Rearranged.

ISLAMORADA, Florida, with Don -- With a burn rate of $10,000 per month on just fixed overhead expenses alone, Don's four years of being retired ate through his money. A windfall here and there extended the time, but he needed some money, and a new contact named Little Mike, introduced by Coconut, wanted to rent the Oasis for a year.

Chelsea had said she never liked Mike from the first second she met him. "He was shifty, and he stumbled over his name when he introduced himself to me. I didn't trust him."

"That could have been because of the halter top you were wearing," said Don alluding to the skimpy clothing Chelsea always *almost* wore.

Little Mike brought marijuana in on a freighter that his boats met in the Bahamas and ferried back to off-load houses in the Keys. He was the flamboyant stereotype of a smuggler that everyone thinks of with the "go-fast boats" making midnight crossings of the Gulfstream at high speed in heavy seas with a load of contraband.

Little Mike needed another off-load house in the Keys and asked if Don would rent him the Oasis. Don said for $100,000 he could have it for a year. "I should have asked for more, a lot more," said Don. Little Mike immediately agreed to the deal.

Kathy's Tom had a trailer in Islamorada and he lived with Kathy by that time, so he had a vacant Keys place, for cheap and Kathy's Tom owed Don for inviting him in to the windfall of $50,000 for the load they had found in front of the Oasis. A deal was made to use the trailer for the year that Little Mike had the Oasis. "I'm not really a trailer kind of girl," said Chelsea with a laugh."

The particular brand of "go-fast" boat that Little Mike used was called a Midnight. It was an improved version of a Cigarette boat hull that was 37 feet long, with a center console and four Mercury Black Max engines. They could do 60 miles per hour if necessary, in six-foot seas with a 7000-pound load and nobody was sure exactly how many of them Little Mike had.

The boats would run back and forth between the freighter in the Bahamas and several off-load houses besides the Oasis,

after which they high-tailed it back to Miami where they cleaned up the boat and got it ready to replace the engines for the next caper.

Don was paid another $10,000 to train the crews to come in the channel and to guide the first trip by radio while monitoring the scanners from a nearby land-locked house.

Little Mike made several successful trips before the drug interdiction authorities added hovercrafts to their arsenal. These could keep up with the Midnights.

For entertainment, Don was listening on the scanner one trip when a hovercraft left Key West to interdict one of the Midnights. Little Mike also told him the story later. It caught up with the boat and shot out the engines. The boat caught fire and slowly sank. The crew members jumped overboard and claimed they didn't know anything about the boat that was on fire sinking nearby.

It ended that scam, but Little Mike had a whole network of distributors to supply and he bought pot from Don for years. "I made him a millionaire from just me," said Don. By the time the first year was up, Little Mike bought his own house about two-blocks from the Oasis and he and Don became close friends and diving buddies who would often hang out together.

Also, by the time the year was up, Don had stopped dating both Chelsea and Jan simultaneously. Chelsea had dropped out of the rotation and Jan was now living with Don full time.

Chapter 41

Tucson Was The Hot New Place To Be.
Bart Was Bringing In Some Excellent, Even
Pretty Mexican Marijuana.

One day Butch called Don and told him he had a guy bringing Mexican weed to Tucson and "it was some really good shit." It was "pretty pot" and it was so good that some guys were sending it by FedEx to Hawaii where retail distributors were selling it on the beach to customers as Maui Wowie or Kona Gold and getting lots of repeat business. "I had a contact in Chicago named Al who was always looking for a good supply, so I checked it out," Don remembered.

"I flew up, rented a car and took 50 pounds to Al. I always sold it for enough that there was at least $100 for me per pound, and I gave Butch another $25 per pound," explained Don. "Al loved it. Over the next year I made about 10 trips of 200 to 300 pounds each.

"Bart was Butch's contact, so I didn't meet him the first couple of trips. He was moving marijuana around using little cars because he used guys as drivers and a guy alone in a big sedan fit a profile. Bart was an odd sort who didn't like to use telephones. He would just show up at your door any time of the day or night, but it always meant fun and profit when he arrived," said Don. "I originally met him in Bloomington and then dealt directly with him, but still paid Butch his $25 per pound. I didn't cut people out of their connections, they were valuable."

The scam went pretty smoothly, with Don's most memorable trip being in the dead of winter when Bart showed up in Bloomington with 200 pounds stuffed in a pickup truck with a tarp over it." Don said, "It's your pot and your truck do you want to risk driving it on the roads under these conditions with a snow storm coming? Bart said 'yes,' so me, a confirmed Keys guy, with no experience driving in that bad of weather headed off to Chicago in a blizzard. The road was slick and in parts of the turnpike it was closed down with only one lane open. It was pretty hairy. I spun around a couple of times but didn't hit anything and didn't go far enough off the road that I couldn't get back on. I inched along to Al's place and when I got there, I was snowed in for three days. It took Al that long to sell the marijuana."

"I stopped doing it because Al didn't pay me $20,000 that he owed on the tenth trip, so we never worked together again," said Don who longed to get into a legitimate business to alleviate the stress of smuggling anyway.

"I opened P&G Automotive as a legal business right after that, with Pat and Gary," said Don. "I funded it, and Pat and Gary were both good mechanics. Pat was the best I've ever known. He had been a mate on the Aqua Sports and worked off-loading the MJ, and had a little marijuana business on the side, but Gary was never part of the business -- although he did develop a coke problem."

"It would take several years to get a business like that going to where it started making money -- we started in 1988 and ran it for four years," remembered Don.

"Pretty soon I started buying marijuana in Tucson and bringing it back to Miami with Debra as the pot driver. She

was a seasoned courier. She had a Volvo that held 200 pounds and it took her three days each way. After a while, we had her boyfriend do the deadhead and flew her to Indiana to drive back."

"We bought a Caprice Classic that would carry 300 pounds and would work on one car while she drove the other," said Don. "We used P & G Automotive to prepare the cars which needed to be worked on every two weeks, so that way it didn't look suspicious like it would have if we had used another legit car repair place."

"I was selling marijuana to Little Mike in quantities of 200 to 300 pounds a month. I sold it for $900 per pound and bought it for about $600 per pound by picking it up in Tucson," remarked Don

That adds up to net profit of about a million dollars for the year, back then, remember inflation kicked that up by two to three times for today's money," said Don. Pat became a partner in this business as well as P&G.

"Debra just drove like a machine and she ate fast food from Burger King. She'd bring the car back and the whole floor of the back seat was filled with Burger King wrappers, bags and cups," remembered Don. "She gained 45 pounds that year."

They marked out the route for Debra. The rule was that she was to drive across I-80 through Memphis across Flagstaff to Phoenix and then down, because there was less heat. "She was not ever supposed to take I-10," said Don, "which goes across the top of Florida, Louisiana and Texas. And she was never supposed to have cocaine in the car!"

"The use of rolled up hundred-dollar bills to snort coke was so common that residue was on just about every bill," said Don. "Remember that court case where the defense attorney said that every hundred-dollar bill would have coke residue on it and the judge told them to check the money in his wallet and sure enough, there was coke residue on each of the judge's hundreds."

"We packed the money to pay for the deal in good quality cellophane wrap with many layers. That much money in hundreds would trigger a drug dog," commented Don. "We would pack the money in the springs under the back seat."

"Well, it was raining, and Debra decided to take I-10 and she had a gram of cocaine for her own use with her. They stopped her in Louisiana for – they said – an illegal lane change, but they were profiling and if they hadn't said 'illegal lane change' they'd have said something else, said Don.

The dog smelled the little bag of cocaine in the ash tray. The police searched the car and found the money. They confiscated the car and the money and arrested Debra. Don said, "It took attorney's fees of $25,000 to get her off and the bust put us out of business.

Next, Pat was in a bad motorcycle wreck and Gary went off to rehab. "It became Don's Automotive as I had to hire some mechanics and work as a manager," said Don. "Pat eventually came back to work, but he was never able to do much again. Gary beat his coke problem and went to work for the Fire Department and lived happily ever after."

"I was out of business at that time, spending much of my time in Homestead and trying to make a legitimate go of the

automotive repair business – getting pretty frustrated with the profits."

Chapter 42

"Can You Introduce Me To Your Connection?" Mike Asked For Don's Connection, He Was Willing To Set Something Up."

Another Day, Little Mike called. "I had been so busy I hadn't talked to him in over a year at that time. We caught up briefly telling each other some of the big things that had happened in our lives since we last worked together. But only *some* of the things," remembers Don.

"Little Mike asked me if I could fix him up with some product and I told him I was pretty much out of that trade now," said Don. So, he asked me if, in that case, I'd introduce him to my Tucson connection for a percentage of each pound. And I said no, because I just didn't want the hassles and stress of the business any more. I was over 50 and fat. And I kind of liked what I was doing, I just wish it had made more money, faster."

Don remembered that "Little Mike offered me $100,000 to introduce him to Bart. He always was too quick to pay $100,000 for something. And I said I would do it." I called Bart and arranged a meeting at the Tucson airport lounge. It was a place where milling about isn't considered loitering, it's just minding your business waiting on a flight.

Bart met me at the airport and we went into the lounge where Mike and his associate Edgar were waiting. I didn't like that Mike had brought someone along, but I trusted him. We chatted briefly. Edgar asked, "How much product can you supply?" It seemed a bit abrupt, as we didn't yet know if he

liked Bart's merchandise. "I gave the standard answer, 'As much as you want.'"

Edgar wanted to talk about specifics of delivery. Don said, "Before we go any further, I'm going to need to see some money. He made a phone call from his cell phone then left for a while. We had lunch and waited for his return. I was about to get tired of waiting – something was wrong with Mike, something didn't feel quite right -- when Edgar came back with a satchel filled with cash. It wasn't enough to cover a load of the 100 pounds they were talking about, but it was a bag of cash and they hadn't seen any pot yet. We arranged when they were going to meet Bart to do the deal."

The time it took to collect the money meant Don missed his return flight and there wasn't another one until the next morning. They concluded the meeting and parted company.

Bart invited Don to stay over at his house and they left for his place, a row house in a middle class, neighborhood with large lots.

Apparently, Edgar's compatriots followed them.

"We walked into Bart's house and within moments the world began to rain agents hollering '*freeze.*'" Mike had been recently busted and was now working as a confidential informant. He had set Don up.

"As the heat came in the front door we went out the back. Bart was an athlete, young and agile, and he got away, said Don. "Like I said, I was 50 and fat with a bad knee, and I didn't make it 20 yards before I fell into a cactus.

Bart got to his car which was parked around the corner and drove 25 hours straight through to show up in Bloomington at Ray's house. He was a bloody mess and Ray

helped him clean up and get presentable to regroup and get on with his life. He got completely away.

Chapter 43

"Mike, Meet Bart."
Or "Violation of Title 21, United States Code,
Sections 841(a)(1) and 841(b)(1)(vii)."

When they bring you out of a jail cell to meet with your attorney and you see the paperwork that says 'UNITED STATES OF AMERICA vs. The name your mom called you when you were in trouble, it is overwhelming. It is like THE ENTIRE FRIGGIN' GOVERNMENT OF THE ENTIRE COUNTRY vs. me. The odds seem stacked.

The Federal Government didn't see the story the same way that Don did. It felt *"that on or about March 4, 1991, to and including April 25th 1991, at or near Tucson in the district of Arizona and elsewhere, the name Don's mother called him and in the same tone as when he was in really big trouble, and Bart (Legal Name Unknown) (Lucky Bastard),*

named herein as defendants and co-conspirators, did knowingly and intentionally combined, conspire, confederate, and agree together and with each other, and with other persons known and unknown to the grand jury to possess with intent to distribute the quantity of marijuana, Schedule I controlled substance, of 100 kilograms or more but less than 1000 kilograms; in violation of title 21, United States code, section 841(a)(1) and 841(a)(1)(B)(vii)."

Count two sounded just as ominous. It said Don had violated the same codes as the first, but also included Title 18 United States code Section 2. It took issue with Don that *he did knowingly and intentionally "possess with intent to distribute and aid, abet, counsel, command, induce, procure and cause others or another to possess with intent to distribute a quantity of 100 kilograms of marijuana."*

They charged Don with over 100 kg, which is over 220 pounds, even though they were talking about a hundred pounds. But Don had said that he could get them all they wanted, and Bart had over 500 pounds in his house.

During the two years it worked its way through the court system before Don was able to plead guilty to reduced charges and forfeit his Homestead house and the Oasis, property worth more than $1 million. They threatened to give him 30 years. He wound up giving up everything, receiving 27 months and had to do 18 months plus the time in a halfway house, and on probation.

Epilogue

Don Adapts To Life In Boys Camp.

"I made ceramics. I turned out to be pretty good at it. I had never done it before, but I figured I had a couple of years to learn. With my mechanical background, I kept the kiln running, at least it wasn't diesel," said Don of his time at "boys camp" in Jessup. It was one of the minimum-security facilities. It was near a wooded area with a railroad track running near the property.

"When I got visitors, I would have them stop by the liquor store and pick up a couple handles of rum and leave them by the railroad track," explained Don. "Next, I had a rabbit, I called him, who would climb the fence that night and retrieve the bottles and fill up empty Tang jars with rum, then climb back in. We split the load fifty-fifty. He was selling his rum for $20 per jar."

"I started buying the rabbit's share because he was getting half the population drunk. One guy drank so much he passed-out and fell down, having thrown-up all over the bathroom. He is lucky he didn't get caught," said Don who next wondered if we had enough stories to make a good book. Then he thought a moment and said about the rumrunning experience, "You had to pace yourself and keep a low profile, so you didn't get caught."

Don remembered with a slight smile, "It was definitely an adventure getting drunk in prison, but, of course, *for adventure there is risk.*"

$ $ $

Smugglers' Times

Smuggling In The Days Of Marijuana Prohibition 1974 to 1992

"True stories in a work of fiction."

As told by Don, Butch and friends
To M. Dennis Taylor

CAST OF CHARACTERS

Characters That Appear More Than Once:

Keys Don: Our protagonist and one of the Partners, also worked under the name Gomer.

Butch: Became friends with Don, Bought the MJ and handled transportation of weed on it.

Peggy: Don's partner in the initial retail pot business and much later his girlfriend.

Bob Z: Peggy's husband

Bear: A supplier who "wanted his money *any way*."

Chili: One of the three Partners. Took to free-basing cocaine, then taking Quaaludes to sleep. At age 35 he went to sleep and never woke up.

Jon B: An American who brought in Colombian pot.

Roger, 'who handled sales:' the craziest of the three Partners. Wore out his nose snorting cocaine and smoked regular cocaine in tobacco cigarettes. Died at 52 of throat cancer.

Bull: Roger knew Bull, who had a connection in Colombia.

The Partners: Don, Chili and Roger.

Linda: Don's girlfriend, he bought her a Corvette and she got wasted and wrecked it.

Piper Cherokee Six: Six-seater, single engine plane.

Hubert, Iggy and Bob: A smuggling group that Roger sold to. They bought Don's first load brought in by single-engine aircraft.

Chateau Lafitte Rothschild, 1970 vintage: Don's favorite wine, "every time I made $100,000, I bought another case."

Cessna 206: Marketed as a station wagon type of aircraft. Six-seater, single engine. Don rented and then bought one.

The Ranch: 40 fenced-in acres, west of Stuart, Florida out by Lake Okeechobee, four miles down a dirt road, with privacy and an airstrip.

Navajo: Modified into "Panthers," a twin-engine Navajo, modified to fly 1100 miles non-stop, and carry one-thousand pounds with only one of its engines running.

Neil, the Whalebone: Ran the off-load crew, Captain on the Terrapins.

The Sweetie Pie: A Sparkman and Stevens-designed, 43-foot, twin diesel engine, steel, single-mast, motor-sailor, which sailed, "but not well."

Terrapin sailboats: Small sailboats used in off-loading and transportation of the pot.

Hollywood Joe: Loaned Butch his power boat to off-load when the Terrapin wound up beached.

CJ: Erratic captain of the Sweetie Pie "about went insane and had to be hospitalized after the trip was over." He ultimately met his end by committing suicide.

Reverend Rick: Mail-order "ordained minister," owned The Marcia Jean.

Marcia Jean: MJ, a purpose-built pot smuggling boat.

Dick: "Had a scale so he got involved to help handle the weigh-in,"

Captain Tim: Captain of MJ for two trips.

Oasis: Property in Islamorada, off-load house for years and more than a dozen capers.

Chris "The Wrench:" Captain of a trip on the MJ, mechanic on the MJ with Captain Tim.

John F: Scary crazy, a bodyguard for some notorious coke dealers. His place was used as a stash house.

John F.'s girlfriend: Yes, she was.

Mr. Florida weight lifter: "Or some such," an erstwhile buddy of John F's, headed toward his own demise.

Otis: Butch's partner in the MJ.

Ray: Butch's brother.

Bo: Bought weed from Butch, they used his place as a stash house.

"Mi Tio:" (My Uncle), out of Santa Marta. Name used on MJ in Colombia, so the boat appeared local, in the waters off Santa Marta.

Captain Paul: Captain of the MJ for one trip.

Captain Dirk: Captain of the MJ, had his nephew and an ex-Coast Guard kid for crew. Partook of way too much cocaine.

Paul and Butch's girlfriends: Chicks made off-duty trips seem legit.

The Old Man: The Colombian connection, the former mayor of Santa Marta whom they called alternately "the old man" or "the spic" depending upon whether they were talking to or about him.

Enrique The Kid: The old man's 20-something-year-old son who ran the marijuana business, and "was a crazy Colombian kid"

"Juan: Don and Chili's surrogate to load the boats in Columbia.

Captain Markus: Captain of Morgan 41 and Morgan 51 sailboat trips.

The Morgan 51 sailboat: Made nearly one trip, was the first boat the Partners owned and the first to get busted.

Chili's Dad: Trusted family member who acted as a surrogate to load the boats for Don and Chili.

Anthony the lawyer: A twitchy, crooked attorney who knew lots of ins and outs and charged dearly for the knowledge.

Abbey the lawyer: Butch's crooked attorney.

Marcus' wife: Had an affair with Chili while Markus was in jail,

Sal: Dealer who showed up at the weigh-in with $100,000 in cash to be first in line to buy.

Aqua Sports: 24-foot Family Fisherman, with twin 140 horsepower Johnson outboards drew less water and faster than Marine Patrol boats of the time.

Red-Headed Chuck: Lost on his own plane trip.

Red-Headed Chuck's girlfriend: Yes, she was, too.

Captain Jim: Notorious Captain that planned to pilot the Golden Eagle but was dying of cancer.

Wolf: Aqua Sport captain.
Pat: Aqua Sport mate.

Tom: Aqua Sport captain.
Tommy: Aqua Sport mate.

Fish: Aqua Sport captain.

Ray: Butch's brother, Aqua Sport mate, Transported weed to Indiana.

Lee Marvin: Academy Award winning actor Lee Marvin, loved fishing and drinking. His wife, or girlfriend sued him for palimony. Star of Cat Ballou.

Lefty: who wasn't actually left-handed, owned a nursery and landscaping business designed and then ran the greenhouse.

Mrs. Lefty: offers a wife in the businesses perspective.

Little Hemi or Roid: Peggy's younger son, appropriately named.

Big Bobby: Peggy's older son, full-time derelict who lived at the grow house and was supposed to be the guard. Collectively he and Hemi were called the Hemorrhoid Brothers.

Scott: ran the Oasis and dealt with many personality types, refused to work with them.

Bassett: worked at the grow house, took a shot over the lowlifes' heads.

Chelsea: Don's girlfriend when he was retired.

Gayle: Bo's ex-wife.

Joanie: married Otis at the Oasis wedding, was later with Buck.

Buck: Distributor of marijuana, a jobber. He bought pot from Butch.

Jan: Don's wild and crazy girlfriend.

Mike: Smuggler who rented Oasis for a year, became good friends with Don.

Gary: Owner of P&G Automotive. Not in the business.

Debra: Driver of marijuana loaded vehicles.

Bart: Supplied Mexican marijuana in Tucson, Arizona.

The Saga Continues in The Next Book:

SMUGGLERS' TIMES:
Smuggling In The Days Of Marijuana Prohibition.

"True stories in a work of fiction."

The Jamaican Scam.

As told by Keys Don and friends
To M. Dennis Taylor

For more information, visit:

www.SmugglersTimes.com

Introduction To

The Jamaican Scam

ISLAMORADA, Florida, with Don -- Like many in his position, after release from prison, Keys Don had aspirations of going straight.

"After I got out of boys camp I went to work for Florida Keys Vending. That's what I was doing for several years until I got off probation and for a while afterwards. I was working a regular job, following all their rules and being a good boy," said Don who had to forfeit everything he had and was sentenced to 27 months. He had to do 18 months incarceration, in addition to time in a halfway house, plus probation and the parting gift of a record that limited options and closed doors all over the place.

This lead to vocations of low pay, hard work and positions of little glamour or excitement. "Being able to fix a vending machine didn't attract wild women like some other things I have done in my life," stated Don.

"One day I heard a knock and Hubert was standing at the front door," remembered Don.

This was Hubert, of Hubert, Iggy and Bob, the successful smuggling group that bought his first loads on the trips in a single-engine plane to bring back pot from Colombia.

"Hubert just showed up at my house one day and said listen 'I got a sailboat with 500 pounds of pot on it, worth a half-million dollars, over in Cozumel and I'll pay you

$100,000 to get it back here and get the load to me,'" remembered Don.

"Hubert explained that the captain and crew had picked up the load in Jamaica and took it to Cozumel and ended up selling the life raft and the sails to buy drugs. Then they hopped on a plane, flew back and abandoned the boat at the dock," said Don. "The Captain was Bull who had flown with me on one, and only one, flight to Colombia," Don said.

"I don't want to say anything about what Bull was," said Don, "But what he was *not* was competent enough to be doing that kind of work. Hubert asked if Don wanted to handle it.

"Fuck yeah," thought Don as he said, "I'll make some calls."

"I started by calling up my old buddies," remembered Don. "I called Pat. I've known Pat since high school and we'd done a lot of work together."

"We had to find a place to off-load the boat, so Pat and I jumped in a car and took about a week to visit every marina between Naples and Tampa.

"We were trying to find a marina where we could pull a sailboat in and off-load 500 pounds of pot. The best one we came across was in Fort Myers. It was not far from the inlet into the marina and there was a tall hotel nearby," explained Don. "We thought it would work out fine. This marina we chose had a lot of sailboats in it and it looked pretty quiet."

They bought supplies to repair the stolen parts of the boat.

Don said, "We ordered the best new sails from Calvert Sails and we spent more than $4000 on a life raft."

"Pat hired a Captain named Bill who had worked for, I'll tell you, it was Roy, another guy we knew well," said Don.

"Bill had a reputation going back years and years of really being a good sailor, but who had done some stupid shit and taken a few chances he probably shouldn't have. He also had a reputation of being a heavy drinker. But, hey, you don't hire teetotaling Ivy League graduates for this job." The rule was always to prohibit cocaine on the boat, and breaking that rule had cost people millions of dollars and more. Now they decided not to allow any alcohol on the trip.

"I didn't know about the decision, but I wouldn't have disagreed," Don said.

Don hired Rixey, who was a guy named Richard, whose last name began with "C," and who liked the odd spelling. They took him to see the marina, so he would be familiar with the area where he was going.

"He was a good guy and a very capable sailor. He knew his way around a sailboat," related Don. "He had no experience with this kind of work. He was going to be the mate and only crew member."

Everyone thought Rixey would be fine in the capable hands of a venerable old salt like Captain Bill.

They took the raft and sails and some supplies to Cozumel where Captain Bill and Rixey checked out the boat. It had been sitting a month, so anybody that was watching it had probably given up and moved on to more pressing cases. They provisioned the boat for a week. On an expense account people are always apt to overbuy, which they did.

"We thought it should take three or four days from Cozumel to Fort Myers," said Don. They didn't have satellite

phones for communication, so they were out of contact with them until they got close and could be picked up using a VHF radio.

Don, Pat and Debra, who had been a driver for the Mexican pot, held up in a high floor of the hotel overlooking the inlet, watching off the balcony, waiting for their ship to come in.

"On the fourth day it wasn't there, five days it wasn't there, six days it wasn't there... On the seventh day we were getting really worried and the boat finally shows up coming in," said Don. "We talked to Rixey on the radio as soon as he got close enough and then we met him at the dock."

Rixey told them what had happened.

Nobody knew how much of a problem drinker Captain Bill was, apparently, not even him. He had gotten sick and started going through alcohol withdrawal on the first day, developed DTs and spent the trip out of his head, sprawled out in the bilge.

"To be that much of a drunk and agree to go four days, cold turkey was a crazy, stupid, dangerous thing to do," said Don.

"He was flat useless," Don remembered. "Worse than useless. He left Rixey to do the entire trip by himself."

Rixey had stayed awake for days, just catching a nap here and there and doing everything that had to be done day and night. "You sail around the clock," stated Don.

On the third night a thunderstorm hit, and it was so strong the howling wind blew the jib off which got caught in the propeller, knocking out the engine.

The boat was just spinning in a circle, screwing itself into the sea. Rixey crawled into the cabin and got himself and Captain Bill into the life raft and literally, holding on for dear life, during the worst nightmare anyone would want to imagine.

The first light of the calm morning found an exhausted Rixey, basically all alone, with an out-of-his-head Captain, on a boat laden with hidden marijuana and no way to sail it or use the motor. It was a good thing he had ample supplies of food and beverages.

Rixey tied a rope to himself and got into the water. Hour-by-hour he cut the strong material from the destroyed new sail from around the screw and prop until he finally had it all free. Using the engine and the main sail, he completed the trip.

Somewhere during the mess, diesel fuel spilled and covered the inside of the boat, the cushions and everything in it, except the pot which wasn't "in" the boat – it was hidden safely within a hollow keel.

"When you're putting a keel on a boat, it is bolted to the boat," explained Don. "There are like three places in the center of the boat where the bolts come up for the keel and it connects onto the boat. Then they fiberglass around that and paint it. Hubert's group did this," Don related.

The special keel would hold the marijuana in a secret compartment that would never be found from inside the boat and looked just like it had been fabricated when the boat was originally built.

"There was a trick to get the plates out even if you had been told they were there. Nobody would have ever have

suspected they were there. With bilge water in it, sniffer dogs wouldn't smell it. They had done a nice job. It was a pretty ingenious way to hide the marijuana by building a bigger keel that was hollow to hold the product," said Don.

We sent Captain Bill home. I had never seen him before and never have seen him since," said Don. We fed him first, we made sure he and Rixey got a good meal at the marina and when we got paid we gave them $20,000 each. Pat paid Captain Bill and said he was drunker than shit when he saw him.

Don said "Debra washed the deck while Rixey worked in the cabin, so she could keep an eye out. She washed the deck for hours as Rixey retrieved the marijuana from its secret compartments and loaded it into sail bags.

Back in the days before the internet, it was a pain in the ass to buy 15 or 20 sail bags. Stores didn't carry that many, so you had to go all over town to find enough," remembered Don.

They loaded the pot in the sail bags into the van and placed the cushions over it. "It really smelled bad from the diesel, we never got that smell out of the van," said Don.

It took half-a-day to get the van loaded and then they had to close up the compartments in case there were any unexpected visitors to the boat.

Then Pat drove in front, Debra in the van with the load and Don in his car behind her. The caravan made its way across Alligator Alley to the stash house and successfully delivered the product.

If she had been stopped for any reason Debra would have been busted," said Don, "the authorities would have had to

investigate the diesel smell." With the marijuana delivered and that portion of the job done, now the boat had to be stowed.

"We were not breaking the law now, but it is always best to avoid any questions from authorities," said Don.

They sailed the boat about three hours away to a marina with a lift that could accommodate it. They had it placed on Hubert's trailer and pulled it with a borrowed dual axel pickup truck. On the drive across Alligator Alley, they got a flat and had to pull into a rest area where Scott waited for two hours with the sailboat with this big, ugly, weird-looking keel, while they went to the Miccosukee Indian Reservation to get the flat fixed.

They towed the boat to a warehouse in Medley that had a parking lot and drive that was too-tight to allow a boat that size to be backed into it.

"It took us nearly forever to get the boat parked in there. Hubert's crew wanted it hidden to get it out of circulation for a while – just let it disappear -- because they didn't know what kind of heat, if any, Bull had brought down on it in Cozumel," said Don.

"It was finally the end of that little caper and the start of The Jamaican scam that went on for years and more than 30 successful, but not smooth trips," said Don. "And I still never brought in cocaine."

When everybody got paid for the little caper, it looked like there would be plenty more where that payday came from. Don thought he knew how to be more careful than in the past -- not be so trusting of deals that seemed not to smell just right.

With plenty of pent-up demand, Don went on an afternoon shopping spree on his way home. He spent thousands at Target and hundreds at specialty shops.

Walking in the door at home he carried in a single bottle of Chateau Lafitte Rothschild, 1970 vintage. Later that evening he had a glass alone, he had broken the inertia to getting back where he knew he belonged.

"I'm back," Don remembered saying as he had a sip of wine he had not tasted in many years. He said with a smile, "My favorite…"

For more information, visit:

SmugglersTimes.com

53784553R00150

Made in the USA
Columbia, SC
23 March 2019